Splash Fields

by

Joseph Cooper

Also by Joseph Cooper

Poetry:

Autobiography of a Stutterer
Touch Me
Arias Let Into
Porlock

Prose:

Talk Like Jazz

Cover image "Cosmic Migration" by Ted Chin (tedslittledream.com)

Cover design by Andrew K. Peterson

Splash Fields ©2024 by **Joseph Cooper**. Published in the United States by Vegetarian Alcoholic Press, Inc. Not one part of this work may be reproduced without expressed written consent from the author. For more information, please write V.A. Press, 643 South 2nd Street, Milwaukee, WI 53204

ISBN: 978-1-952055-56-0

for Emily

Table of Poems

The Current	1	The Waiting Room	56
The Sleeping Man	2	The Sky	57
Imaginary Pistol	4	The Brown Bear	59
Golden Locket	5	Digging	61
Meet-Cute	6	The Drawbridge	63
Flying	8	The Instruction Manual	65
The Choreographer	10	A Real Family	66
The Track Star	12	The Woods	68
The Werewolf	14	The Rope	69
Rush Hour	16	The Happy Pistoleer	71
The Family Reunion	18	The Mirepoix	73
The Fisherman	20	The Zen Garden	74
The Soldier	22	Mother	76
The First Chapter	23	Let it Snow	77
The Stenographer	25	The Supermarket	79
The Tornado	27	A New Man	80
The Dead Man	29	Kissing Dynamite	82
The Little Guy	31	The Disappearing Act	84
The Kirkland Bird Club	33	A Wonderful World	86
The Honeybee	35	The Medicine Cabinet	87
The State Fair	37	A Bottomless Freefall	89
The Attic	39	A Gentleman's Club	90
The American Bison	41	The Carolers	91
The Unicorn	42	The Adventures of	
Santa Claus	45	Martin George	92
Lucky Penny	47	Glowing	93
The Rooster	49	The Player Piano	94
The Village	52	History	95
The Clicking Sound	54	Linus	96

*"No live organism can continue for long to exist sanely
under the conditions of absolute reality."*
—Shirley Jackson

The Current

Sharon pointed out over the water at two people making love while the current swept them away. "They're in love," she said. "How can you tell?" I said. "You can tell by the way the river is taking them briskly out to sea." "They look like they're drowning," I said. "No, silly," she said, placing her head on my shoulder. "They're definitely making love. Look at the way she comes up for air, how he reaches out to her for support, the way their bodies writhe against the ebb and flow." I thought I heard one of them calling for help, but I didn't want to spoil the mood. "How come we never make love like that?" I said. "Like what?" she said. "Like we're about to die," I said. "We're not really water people," said Sharon. "I mean, when we go to the beach we only go in up to our ankles." "We like to hike," I said. "What if we made love while fighting off a mountain lion?" "I don't know," said Sharon. "We could even go next weekend," I said. "There's supposed to be a really low chance of rain."

The Sleeping Man

As I made my way among the other guests, I couldn't help but fall in love with a painting of a sleeping man. His head rested in his arms as if it belonged to someone else. It was illuminated by a single light, which attracted the attention of several partygoers. A man leaned into me and asked, "What's it called?" "I call it *The Sleeping Man*, but I guess it's open to interpretation," I said. "I'll give you five hundred dollars for *The Sleeping Man*," he said. "Oh, I don't live here," I said. "I understand, there is life beyond art," he said. "But no one would begrudge you if you did." "No, that's not what I meant at all," I said. "Now you're being either modest or coy, I can't really be sure," he said. "I know, it's so charming," said an older woman. "I'll give you a thousand for *The Sleeping Man*." "No, really, you don't understand," I said. "That's a rather provincial attitude," she said. "You have gusto! I like that. I'll give you two thousand." Then a man rushed out of the bathroom, still zipping his fly, threw his arm around me and said, "I'm the one, I represent the artist." "I don't even know you," I said. "All artists are the same," said a man twisting his mustache. "Not this one," said my agent. "In that case, I'll give you five thousand dollars for *The Sleeping Man*," said the mustachioed man. "Please," I said, "this is my first time even seeing this painting." "I know," said a young woman eyeing me flirtatiously. "It's amazing how you can spend weeks, months, even years working on a piece and somehow when it's on a gallery wall it seems so foreign." "Yes, yes," said a smoking man. "You're so convincing in your distance from the work. I'd almost believe it was your first encounter with *The Sleeping Man*. I'll give you ten thousand dollars and a contract for your future paintings." "There's been some kind of mistake," I said. "I'm not an artist." "No one would ever dream of pigeonholing you," said my agent. Then he handed the smoking man a slip of toilet paper stuck to his shoe. "Here's my card," he said. "We'll discuss the contract first thing in the morning." "I have to work," I said. "That's the spirit,"

said the smoking man. "With that attitude you're going to be famous,
and we're all going to be filthy rich." Then someone put on a record
and there was dancing. Everyone was bumping and grinding against
each other. Barefoot women held their heels in their hands. Men swung
their sportcoats overhead like lassos. "You're going to be a star,"
said my agent. He mingled with the crowd and began dancing. The girl
giving me eyes continued giving me eyes until I asked her to dance.
Then all the lights went out except for the one illuminating the sleeping man.
"This is a wonderful exhibition," said a fashionable couple dancing past us.
"You really are magnificent," said an older woman holding a chihuahua.
After a few songs, it appeared as if everyone were suddenly dancing in
a wind tunnel, their hair and clothing whipping from side to side
while the sound of music was muffled by a colossal storm. "You
really know how to throw a party," someone shouted. Then a window
shattered outward into the night and people were gradually sucked
into the beyond. Many of them laughed and reached for each other,
for anything to hold onto. "This is the party of the year," said a man,
losing his toupée. "No," said his wife, "the century." Even the sleeping
man, holding his head as if he were holding another man's head, sat up
and began to sway back and forth, set helplessly adrift
into the limitless margins of abstraction.

Imaginary Pistol

The night I came out of the bedroom naked holding an imaginary pistol to my head, Angela became stricken with grief. "I thought we were past all this," she said. "I mean, everything's been going so well." "I'm sorry," I said. "I'm afraid it's all too much. I can't go on pretending anymore." "Maybe if we did a marionette and puppeteer arrangement?" "I've already thought about that," I said. "It won't work." "Have you considered building a fort out of the couch cushions and using the blue throw blanket as a moat?" "It wouldn't change anything," I said. "And besides, it's too risky." "There's got to be something we can do," said Angela. "Not unless you're willing to play elevator again?" "I just couldn't," said Angela. "Not anymore. Maybe if you'd asked me last week, but not now." "Robot?" I said. "I don't think so," she said. "We could start a band using household materials?" I said. "You could play the pots, or the rubber-band banjo." "No Alan, I'm sorry, we're just not on the same page right now. What if there was an imaginary art gallery?" said Angela. "What about Santa's Workshop?" I said. "Maybe you're in a grocery store and I'm a helpful cashier?" said Angela. "We could build cereal box laptops?" I said. "No, no," she said. "It just won't work." "There's only one thing left to do then," I said. So, Angela went into the bedroom, took off her clothes and folded them neatly on the bed. Then she opened her closet and removed an imaginary shotgun from the top shelf. She cocked it, turned quickly and fired. I fell backward over the coffee table and collapsed on the floor. I felt like an avalanche at the edge of a cliff. I tried to raise my imaginary pistol to defend myself, but Angela rushed into the living room and kicked the gun out of my hand. Then she stood over me, cocked her shotgun again, and finished the job.

A Golden Locket

Once we reached the dock, Rosemary and I unloaded the skiff and set out on the water. "I hope we get lucky," she said. "*Shh*," I said, "we don't want to scare them off." "I know, I know," said Rosemary. "I'm just so excited. I still can't believe more people don't know about this spot." I baited Rosemary's hook with a golden locket and she cast it out into the lake. Then I fastened an action figure onto my line and sent it whirling in the other direction. I cracked a couple of beers and we waited. After a few minutes went by I felt a tug. "I got one, I got one," I muttered. I dragged the line closer and closer. "Don't lose it," said Rosemary, wiping away a tear. Then the line broke and I fell backward into the boat. "Darn it!" I said, "that one was going to be special. We almost had it." "It's okay," said Rosemary, "we'll get one sooner or later. We just need to be patient." "I'm tired of being patient," I said. "Everyone always says, *be patient. It's God's will*. I've had enough." I started retying my line with a matchbox car when Rosemary groaned and nearly fell into the water. "Oh my God, it's happening!" she shouted. "It's really and truly happening! You better get over here, Dusty, this is a big one. Get the net." I grabbed the net and together we dragged the catch into the boat. "Oh my God, Dusty, would you look at that!" We pulled back the netting and found three little blonde girls clothed in floral summer dresses fighting over the golden locket. "Congratulations," said Rosemary, wiping the sweat off her brow. "You're a father!"

Meet-Cute

"So, how did you guys meet?" asked our new neighbor Kathy. "Oh, you don't want to hear that story," said Gertrude. "That's a *story*," I said. "Yeah, no, honey, they don't need to unpack all that," said Kathy's husband Edgar. "Why not?" said Kathy. "I love hearing how couples meet. I'm kind of an aficionado of meet-cutes." "Alright, alright," I said, "but it's nothing spectacular, just the way most couples meet, I suppose." "Everyone's story is beautiful in its own way," said Kathy. "Okay, well, it was early spring and uh, do you want to tell it?" I said. "You tell it," said Gertrude, smiling. "I love the way you tell it. It's so much more romantic when you tell it with all the details that I somehow forget." Gertrude placed her hand on my knee and winked at our guests. "Okay, well, like I was saying, it was early spring," I said. "May, if I remember correctly," said Gertrude. "I think you're right," I said, "because the peonies were in full bloom." "It sounds perfect already," said Kathy, interjecting. "It really was a lovely time of year to meet," said Gertrude. "So, what happened next?" said Edgar, chiming in. "Let's see," I said. "I was going for a jog in Tanglewood Park, just one of those things I'd be doing any old day of the week. I remember jogging along the trail really early in the morning, nobody else out yet, and just moments after I'd started, an enormous owl, must have been a great horned owl, swooped down out of nowhere. Nearly scared my soul right out of me." "Wow," said Edgar, "that must have been quite a sight." "It was," I said. "Truly amazing." "Really is," said Kathy, "but I still want to hear about when you met this ray of sunshine." "Of course," I said. "Well, I gathered my wits about me and kept jogging, and it's a good thing I did because when I turned the corner to follow the trail around the lake, there she was," I said, lifting Gertrude's hand to my lips to kiss it. "Oh my," said Kathy. "Did you have a cramp or injure yourself in some way? Let me guess, Ezra lifted you up in his big, strong arms and carried you to safety." "Something like that," said Gertrude. "So, what did you see?" said Edgar. "The love of my life," I said. "She had taken down this enormous buck, must have been an eight-pointer, and she was just tearing him apart with her bare hands. She saw me approaching and lifted her head from his lifeless body, blood pouring down her chin and chest. You should have seen it, like Cupid's entire quiver had been emptied on her." I pulled Gertrude close and kissed her forehead. "That's when she smiled at me, little bits of flesh and fur between her teeth, and reached into the buck's chest cavity and ripped out his heart. I'd never seen anything quite so sensual, dare I say, erotic. Then she took a bite of it, and threw it to me. I took a bite, two steps forward, and threw it back. This went on for several minutes until we were standing a foot apart and had consumed the entire heart. Together we dragged the carcass deep into the woods and there made love for days without speaking. It actually wasn't until we found a quiet stream and washed off the blood that we introduced ourselves," I said. "Isn't that right darling?" "It is," said Gertrude unbuttoning the top button of her blouse. "From that very moment," I said, kissing Gertrude softly on her lips, "I knew my search was over, that she was the one with which I would spend the rest of my life."

Flying

One day I was driving through the cornfields of Nebraska when I noticed a sign that read "$3 FOR 3 MINUTES IN THE AIR!" I slowed to a crawl. There were no other cars in sight in any direction. *Maybe I'm the only one left*, I thought. I turned off the road onto a dirt path between the cornstalks. I drove for several minutes before rounding a bend and slamming my brakes in front of an old-timey ticket booth. It had sliding glass windows inscribed with the word "TICKETS" in big bubble letters. I sat there for a moment and looked around. I was a little nervous, and even thought about throwing the car in reverse and getting the hell out of there. There was a girl in the ticket booth staring impatiently at me like she'd been waiting for me all day. She blew a bubble with her chewing gum. Then another. And another. After the third bubble, I got out of the car and walked up to the booth. "One?" she said. Her eyeliner was beginning to bleed from the heat. "Please," I said. "Three dollars," she said. I counted out three singles and slid them beneath the glass partition. She tore off a ticket and slid it across the counter toward me. "You're all set," she said. "Now just follow the stalks into the open field." "What's out there?" "You want to fly, don't you?" She seemed annoyed with me so I just replied, "Of course." "Well, then follow the stalks into the open field." She blew another bubble and put up a sign that said "Back in 15" and then she stepped out of the ticket booth and disappeared into the corn. I followed the cornstalks and when I reached the open field, there stood a very tall man beside a platform with three steps. He must have been over seven feet tall. We stood there staring at each other for several seconds until I held up my ticket and he nodded gently. "Come, come," he said, waving me over. I walked over and handed it to him. He gestured to the platform. "Come, come," he said. He took my hand and helped me up the three steps. "Are you ready?" he said. "I think so," I said. He turned to his side and held out his arms. "Lay across my arms," he said. I took a deep breath and laid across his arms. "Now reach your arms out," he said. I reached my arms out long and wide. Then he slowly spun me around and around the open field while making little propeller noises with his mouth, raising and lowering me slightly with the turbulence. After a minute he reached cruising altitude and said, "Wave to your neighbors." "This is amazing," I said, waving to my neighbors. "I always swore I'd do this one day." "And now you have," he said, smiling and beginning his descent.

The Choreographer

Walking into town today, I had the instinctive feeling that I was about to be murdered. I kept looking over my shoulder, squinting into the distance, and making sudden movements to catch the murderer off guard. I'd throw a leg backward, chop erratically, tumble through the grass, leap and spin in the air, then shout something outrageously random like, "*Turnip greens make a great salad!*" or "*Beach ball bouquets bubble up out of boutonnieres!*" It became something of a choreographed dance: kick, jump, spin, chop, squat, tumble, lunge, and shout. Kick, jump, spin, chop, squat, tumble, lunge, and shout. A young woman jogging along the road stopped beside me and tapped me on the shoulder. "Say the moves out loud," she said. I hesitated. "What if you're the murderer?" I said. "I'm not the murderer," she said. "I just want to dance." "Alright," I said. "It goes like this. Kick, jump, spin, chop, squat, tumble, lunge, and shout." "Say it again," she said. "Kick, jump, spin, chop, squat, tumble, lunge, and shout," I said. "Okay," she said. "I think I've got it." We continued down the road until a businessman dropped his briefcase on the ground and joined us. A woman mailing letters at a mailbox threw her letters into the air and joined us. Dozens of old men playing chess in the park stopped playing chess in the park and joined us. A middle-aged couple arguing in front the courthouse stopped arguing and joined us. An old farmer standing in front of the hardware store threw his new rake into his flatbed and joined us. All the shops emptied and the patrons and employees and managers joined us. All the offices emptied and all the office workers joined us. All the factories emptied and all the factory workers joined us. All the children ran out of school screaming and joined us. Kick, jump, spin, chop, squat, tumble, lunge, and shout. Kick, jump, spin, chop, squat, tumble, lunge, and shout. When we reached the outskirts of town, I accidentally kicked, jumped, spun, chopped, squatted, tumbled, lunged, and shouted into a boobytrap in the ground. No one heard me

kick, jump, spin, chop, squat, tumble, lunge, and shout.
I tried again to kick, jump, spin, chop, squat, tumble, lunge,
and shout my way out of the boobytrap in the ground,
but there was nothing I could do. The crowd
knew all my moves and quickly headed out of town.

The Track Star

I was changing the cat litter when I heard someone's muffled cries for help. I stood up and looked around the room. I listened for a moment to the silence. I figured I was hearing things, so I went back to scooping litter. Then I heard it again, this time more clearly: the sound of a man's voice calling for help. I looked out of the window and squinted into the light. "Help," said the voice. I pressed my ear to the screen. "Please help," said the voice. "Oh hell," I said. "This is ridiculous. Where are you, voice?" The voice went quiet. I went back to emptying the cat litter. As I reached the bottom of the litter box, I heard the voice again. "Oh, thank God," said a little man dressed in a tracksuit. He climbed to the rim and dusted himself off. "Thank God," he said again. "I thought I was going to die in there." I stood there slack-jawed and rubbing my eyes. "You're probably wondering how I ended up in there," he said pointing to the litter box. I nodded. "Well, I was taking my usual morning run around your living room, really trying my best to beat my record when all of a sudden, a masked man with a lead pipe jumped out the of bookshelf and demanded money. He scared the hell out of me. I don't usually carry money on my person when I jog, but I was headed to the coffee shop so I was wearing my fanny pack. And with my headphones on it was a total surprise. Anyway, he chased me all around the house, under the couch, behind the toaster, even across the piano keys until I finally lost him in the litter box. I buried myself in there as far as I could dig. It was demeaning as all hell, but I didn't want to die. I imagine most people would do just about anything to avoid death. After a little while your cat came over," he said, wiping his brow and shaking litter out of his tennis shoes. "Slippers?" I said. "Yeah," he said, "Slippers. Slippers started kicking around and buried me even deeper. Fortunately, I found an air pocket amidst the refuse. All I can say is, thank God you played hooky today from work. I might have been a goner if I had to wait until tonight." "I didn't play hooky," I said. "I'm just under the weather." "Maybe so," he said, "but you better watch your ass. That masked man is still out there somewhere."

The Werewolf

I poured a cup of coffee and walked over to the window to watch the sunrise. On my lawn was a naked man lying on his back with blood on his mouth, chin, and chest. I sipped my coffee, sighed, and thought about calling the police but then he sat up, rubbed his head and started looking around. When he saw me at the window he smiled and waved. I smiled and waved back. Then he gestured to me requesting a cup of coffee. He stood up, dusted himself off, and walked to the front door. "Oh man," he said. "What a night. Where the hell am I?" "The suburbs of Cleveland," I said. "No kidding?" he said. "I'm afraid not," I said. "Would you like to come inside?" I said. "Yes, please," he said. "What happened to you?" I asked as I led him into the kitchen. "Are you alright? Do you need me to call someone?" "No, I'm fine," he said. "I could just really use a cup of coffee." "How do you take it?" I said. "Cream and a little sugar," he said. I fixed a cup and handed it to him. "Sweet baby Jesus," he said. "That's good." "I think so," I said. "After drinking terrible coffee for years, I finally sprang for the good stuff, and it was worth it." "I'll say," he said. A few minutes went by and I said, "I can't help but notice that you're naked and covered in blood." "Is it obvious?" he said. "I'm afraid so," I said. He scratched his head and asked for a refill. When I gave him his coffee he said, "You wouldn't happen to have a towel and maybe some cheap old clothes I could borrow, would you?" "Hell," I said, "take a shower and I'll pick out something really nice for you to wear." "Thank you," he said. "You're a real gentleman." "My pleasure," I said. "It's not every day someone wakes up on your front lawn naked and confused." "Don't forget covered in blood," he said, smiling. "I couldn't possibly," I said, patting him on the back. When he got out of the bathroom, I offered him my old wedding tuxedo. "What do you think?" I said. "I don't have any use for it anymore now that my wife has passed." "It's glorious," he said. "I can really see myself in this." He dressed and brushed his hair and I walked him to the door. Before he left, I slipped him twenty bucks and the car keys and said, "Don't stay out too late, son."

"Oh, I won't, Pop," he said. I blew him a kiss and watched him drive away.

Rush Hour

I was stuck on the 198 in bumper-to-bumper rush
hour traffic driving home from work under the hot sun
when I noticed an old man in the car next to me. He was
wearing red long johns and holding a pair of binoculars
to his eyes, looking out into the endless line of vehicles.
Then he let the binoculars drop to his chest and he reached
for a large canteen to take a drink. He screwed the
cap back on and wiped his mouth on his sleeve.
He vigorously ruffled his hair, shifted his hatchback
into park, climbed out, and stretched toward the sun.
He opened up the trunk and climbed into a pair of grizzled jeans,
a flannel, some work boots, and an old straw hat. After a moment,
he noticed me staring at him and waved. "Morning," he said.
"Looks like it's going to be a fine day." "Morning?" I said. My watch
read 5:12 p.m. "I beg your pardon, but I didn't see you over there.
Didn't realize I camped so close to you." "Um," I said, "it's no
problem." "You're welcome to join me for a cup of coffee
if you'd like," he said. "Maybe even some breakfast if the creek's
feeling generous. Just give me a minute to get a fire going."
"Breakfast?" I said. He blew hot breath into his hands and
rubbed them together. "For as long as I've been doing this, I still
never get over the cold." "The cold?" I said. The temperature gauge
in my car read 82 degrees. After several minutes he got a fire going.
"I'm going to step down to the creek for a piss and some fresh water
to boil for coffee. See if we can't get a bite. Would you mind keeping
an eye on the fire, maybe add a log if she needs it?" "Sure, no problem,"
I said, getting out of my car and stepping toward the fire. "I'm Rudy,"
said the man, tipping his old straw hat and extending his hand."
"Michael," I said. "Much obliged, Michael," he said before walking off
toward the median with his empty coffee pot. He leaped over it
as if he were leaping over a log in the woods. I rolled up my sleeves
and removed my tie. I felt in that moment, just as surely as I could smell
the car exhaust choking the air, that I was out in the middle of nowhere.
I smiled, then added another log and poked at the ashes. I heard whistling
and out from behind a sputtering minivan came Rudy. When he saw me,

he said, "Nothing like a morning piss in the woods." Rudy nuzzled the coffee pot into the hot ashes. "Hope you like trout," he said, flopping half a dozen onto a rock and removing a hunting knife from a sheath on his hip. "It's been a while, but yes," I said. I watched him clean the trout quickly and easily, as if he'd been doing nothing but cleaning trout his entire life. As he finished, he looked up at me. "How long you been traveling?" said Rudy. "I'm not really sure," I said. "Must be a while to lose track like that," he said. "Me? I've been on the road forever. Lost track ages ago. Never thought much to settle down. Well, I was in love once, but she didn't feel the same." "I'm sorry," I said. "Don't be," he said. "If she would have felt the same, I would have lost all this," he said, gesturing to all the vehicles starting and stopping, starting and stopping.

The Family Reunion

Blanche looked at her reflection and her reflection looked back at her and said, "Get out there, darling, before all that's left of you is your mother." She reapplied her lipstick, kissed her reflection, and reached for the doorknob. Then a young man, covered in bloody scratches and teeth marks and dressed in a torn-up suit, burst through the door before she could open it. He locked the door and cowered between the toilet and the wall, breaking out in sobs. "Judy," he said. "Oh, my sweet Judy." "What seems to be the matter?" Blanche said. "Judy," he said. "She's gone. I don't know where," he whimpered. "But she's gone." Blanche reached for the doorknob. "I'm sure wherever she is, young man, we can find her." "Don't, don't," he said. "Don't open that door." "Why in heavens not?" said Blanche. "It's a jungle out there," he said. He wiped away tears with his blood-stained hands. "What do you mean, a jungle?" said Blanche. "It's just a party, sweetheart." Blanche reached for the doorknob again. The young man stood up and blocked the door. "No, don't," said the young man. "Don't do it, ma'am. Please don't." Blanche leaned against the vanity and looked at her reflection. "What's your name, sweetie?" Blanche said, winking at her reflection. "Oliver," he said. "Oliver, you must be Judy's boyfriend. I'm her great aunt Blanche. It's nice to meet you." Oliver smiled through his tears. "How old are you, Oliver?" "I'm 23," he said. "Now tell me Oliver, why are you so afraid of going out there?" "I told you already," he said. "It's a jungle out there." "There aren't that many guests out there," said Blanche. "Certainly not enough to call it a jungle." "I literally saw an old man get his head ripped off by a lion," said Oliver. "I've never been more terrified in my entire life." "I know life can be difficult, Oliver. It might even seem like a jungle. But rest assured, you're not the only one who feels a little crazy at these reunions. They make us all a little batty." "No," said Oliver, "you don't understand, I'm bleeding, for Christ's sake. People are dying out there." "Is that a hickey on your neck, Oliver?" "No ma'am," he said. "Don't be embarrassed, Oliver," said Blanche. "Even I've had

my share of romances. Some more vigorous than others."
"It's not like that," said Oliver. "A boa constrictor
tried to kill me, but somehow, I got away and…"
"Oh," said Blanche, "I think Victor is at the piano.
Come on Oliver, it's time for a little song and dance."
"I don't think we should," said Oliver. "Nonsense,"
said Blanche. "Now tuck in your shirt. Brush back your hair.
Fill your lungs with the sound of music." "Blanche, I just can't,"
said Oliver. "Turn and look at your reflection," said Blanche.
"Repeat after me," she said. "Get out there before all that's left of
you is your mother," said Blanche's reflection. "Get out there before
all that's left of you is your mother," said Oliver's reflection.
"Now put on your best face and get ready to sing your little heart out."

The Fisherman

When I went out to water my garden, there was a middle-aged man sitting in an inflatable raft preparing to cast his rod. "No luck today," he said. "I couldn't buy me a bite if I was baiting with silver dollars." "You can't fish here," I said. "This is my flower garden." "Whatever it is," he said, "it's a pretty awful fishing spot. I'll be seeing you." Then he took his oars and began paddling at the grass. The boat didn't move, but he really worked up a sweat. After a few minutes he stopped, took off his hat, and wiped off his face. He opened a cooler and took out a tuna fish sandwich and a cold beer. "Now this is what I call living," he said. When he had finished his sandwich and beer, he fixed his bait and recast into my azaleas. "Those are my azaleas," I said. "Listen buddy," he said, "if you're going to be out on the water, you're going to need to keep it down. You're scaring away all the fish." I turned on the hose and started watering my garden. "Darn it," he said. "They weren't calling for any rain today." The fisherman reeled in his line and opened another beer. "Just going to have to wait it out, I guess," he said. I finished watering and wound up the hose. The fisherman had already recast into my rose bushes. As I walked back to the house, Dan from next door called me over. "Hey Jerry," he said. "I see you got a little fisherman infestation." "Yeah," I said. "He's got a cooler too, so I don't suppose he'll be heading out for a while." "A buddy of mine," said Dan, "had an issue last month with a fisherman. Actually, it was a whole group of them. He figured he'd wait it out too, but after the fishermen cleared out their coolers, they docked at his back door and joined him and his family for dinner. Over the next week they ate all his food, drank every drop of alcohol in the house, and just loafed around belching and farting all day long. They made a real mess. He finally called an exterminator and it was still days before they packed up their gear and left." "Really?"

I said. "That sounds terrible, just terrible." "I know you only have one fisherman right now," he said, "but if I were you, I wouldn't wait too much longer before I called for assistance. Even one can be tricky, and he's already looking mighty comfortable."

The Soldier

"Wake up, Sir!" said a balding man with a pencil mustache. "Mr. Marshall is waiting for you in the conservatory." I startled awake and pulled the covers up to my chin. "I know, I know, *'where am I, who are you, what's going on,'* the same old story. Well, I'm afraid we don't have time for the *'where am I, who are you, what's going on'* routine. You need to get dressed immediately and get downstairs. I've laid out your clothes and he's expecting you shortly." "Who?" I said. "Mr. Marshall," he said, getting so close to my face I could smell his aftershave. "Now pull yourself together and get downstairs at once." He left the room and closed the door. I stood up and ran into the bathroom. I opened the window and looked outside. There was a young woman sweeping the walkway. "Hello," I said. "Up here." The young woman looked around and located me. "Sir?" she said. "I need your help," I said. "I don't know where I am." "Sir?" she said, again. Then an older woman barked at her and she hurried off to continue sweeping elsewhere. Seeing no alternative, I dressed in the clothes laid out for me and walked down a long winding staircase onto the main floor. "Good to see you've risen, Sir," said another man. "Can I get you any coffee? Something to eat?" said another. "Coffee," I said. "Wonderful," said the first man. "Leland will bring your coffee to the conservatory. This way, Sir." We reached the conservatory and when he opened the door, there was a little boy pacing up and down the walkway blowing bubbles with bubblegum. "Mr. Marshall?" said the man. "Mr. Barrymore to see you." "Finally," said the boy, dropping to one knee to bounce a ball and collect all his jacks in one fell swoop. "Mr. Barrymore," he said, "we are at odds with the universe. Everything is changing faster than I can control. We need to figure this out as soon as possible. Otherwise, all will be lost." He continued speaking, but rather than words, I heard what sounded like a small plane losing altitude. Then there was a tiny explosion and a thin, wavering line of smoke rising from between some purple peonies. It wasn't until the boy shook my hand that I noticed the wisping descent of a white parachute and a soldier with a look of terror in his eyes as he floated passed my face.

The First Chapter

I was feeling a little out of sorts, and even though it was raining I decided to take a walk. I put on my yellow raincoat and my black rainboots and walked east on Hamilton. As I walked, I noticed that every other house I passed, someone would exit the front door wearing a yellow raincoat and black rainboots and start walking along the road in the rain. After a few blocks I took a left on Cayuga and they all followed behind me. Then I continued down Washington in the direction of city hall. There were so many of us that we filled the entire street. Up ahead I noticed that the police had assembled roadblocks so that we could peacefully traverse. There were people behind the police blockades shouting profanities and throwing garbage at us as we walked. When I turned to avoid a head of browning lettuce, I saw that there were hundreds, maybe thousands of people marching with me, all wearing yellow raincoats and black rainboots. Some had even begun waving signs in the air that read: *Out of Sorts, Down in the Dumps, A Little at Loose Ends.* Many of them were blotting tears with their wet raincoats and blowing their noses into damp handkerchiefs. As we passed the courthouse, the police were having difficulty holding back the angry mob. "We're just a little sad today," I said to a woman who held up a child so he could throw a tomato at me. "Everyone has bad days now and again," I said to a man who lunged to grab my yellow raincoat and narrowly missed. Then a church bell chimed and the mayor exited the town hall and stood at a podium in a yellow raincoat and black rainboots. The angry mob was horrified by what they saw and began to growl and snarl like animals. Others were too dumbstruck to speak. The police blew their whistles, raised their batons, and pushed the angry mob back behind the blockades. Then the mayor tapped the microphone and began to speak. "Welcome, everyone. Thank you for joining us. This has been an emotional journey for us all, I know. And though many of you would rather persist in the most inauthentic joy than admit to the inevitable transience of our emotions, I hereby declare April 17 be recognized as the saddest day there has ever been, and henceforth the saddest day there ever will be in the history of our great community." Then the mayor began crying into the microphone. His sobs echoed through the crowd and as they did so, all of his aides and security broke down, too. Everyone in the angry mob began to sob in each other's arms. Even the police officers wept and reached out to embrace the other officers. Their dogs howled to the sky and the rain slowly began to dissipate. Then a young woman wearing a yellow raincoat and black rainboots walked up to me and took my hand. She pulled back her hood and smiled. And that is how my affair with Astrid Bressett began.

The Stenographer

On my way to work this morning, I noticed a stenographer was tailing me. I stopped for a cup of coffee and a scone and there she was behind me, clamoring away on the keys. I bought a newspaper at a stand and she jotted down every bit of small talk. Even when I bumped into a young woman walking her Schnauzer and apologized for my clumsiness, the stenographer didn't miss a beat. She sat in the corner throughout all my meetings, looking around the room while her fingers tapped away. She was there with me on the basketball court after work, and even in the grocery store where I stopped to pick up a few things. That night, Rachel came over and I made her dinner. About halfway through the meal, she wiped her mouth and said, "What's with the stenographer?" "I'm not really sure," I said. "She started following me on my way to work this morning. She didn't seem to belong to anyone so I just let her tag along." "Did you check her purse? Maybe she has a home," she said. "Someone probably misses her." "I thought about it, but I just didn't feel comfortable digging through her personal belongings." "I'm sure she won't mind," said Rachel. She stood up and walked over to the stenographer who had, of course, recorded our entire conversation. "Now, I'm just going to check your purse really quick, okay?" she said. "I just want to see if there's anyone out there who's wondering where you are." The stenographer took one hand off her typewriter and shoved her purse underneath her arm. "Don't worry, sweet lady," said Rachel. "I just need to see where you belong." The stenographer typed every word one-handed and then sharply slapped Rachel's hand. "I don't think she likes you," I said. "Maybe *you* should try," she said. "Don't worry about it," I said. "We'll figure it out in the morning. Even if we find something, there's nothing we can do until tomorrow. Have another glass of wine. Just let her type, she's not doing any harm." "Alright," she said. After we finished dinner and another bottle of wine, Rachel and I started kissing on the couch. I began unbuttoning her blouse and telling her how beautiful she was and how I'd been looking forward to this moment all week. "Wait," said Rachel. "Can we put the stenographer outside?" "It's raining," I said. "I can't put her outside. That would be cruel." "Let's go to the bedroom then. At least we'll be in the dark." In the bedroom I got her blouse off and began pulling at her skirt. "Say something dirty." "What?" said Rachel. "Say something dirty," I said. "No, I can't," she said. "Why not?" I said. "I'm too embarrassed," she said. "Why?" I said. "Because it'll be on record," she said. "Don't worry about it," I said. "I've said plenty of awful things today and they're all on record." I licked her neck and left a trail of kisses down her body. Rachel moaned and rubbed her hands through my hair. She started talking dirty, shyly at first, but after a while she completely lost herself in it, saying things I never imagined I would hear. It was as though she had forgotten entirely about the stenographer vigorously typing at the foot of the bed. At one point I even thought I heard the stenographer gasp, but it was probably just the swift return of the carriage.

The Tornado

The local news said a tornado was imminent
and to seek shelter immediately, but I hadn't been
on a date in over a year so I took my chances.
I arrived at the restaurant, narrowly missed by
a few fallen branches, downed power lines,
and a flying mailbox. The winds were really
picking up and several customers had already
rushed to their cars to avoid the storm, holding
onto each other and their belongings for dear life.
I hurried inside and flagged down the hostess,
who was slipping into her coat and shouldering
her purse. "Hello there," I said. "I'm supposed to
be meeting someone here. Do you happen to know
if she's arrived?" "I don't know, mister," she said,
"but I don't think anyone's coming out on a day like
this." She pulled up her hood and ran to her car.
After a few moments of the waitstaff ignoring me
to help older customers into their coats
and out of the building, I was able to flag down
a buxom middle-aged woman standing by the register.
"Excuse me," I said. "Are you the manager?" "I surely
am," she said, stapling receipts and locking the register.
"That hostess was very rude to me just now. I have a date
tonight in your establishment and I'm simply trying to find
out whether or not she's arrived." "Sir, I apologize for
our hostess, but have you heard the news?" "What news?"
I said. "About the tornado?" she said. "Oh, that news,
of course, I've heard that news, but why on Earth
should news of a tornado keep me from the probability
of true love?" "I'm sorry, sir, but I'm afraid we're closing,"
she said. "Closing?" I said. "You can't close. I'm meeting
a young woman. We're going to fall in love, get married,
have children, grow old together. It's going to be miraculous."
"Again, I apologize sir, but there's really nothing
I can do about it," she said. Then the fire marshall came in

and said everyone needed to evacuate as soon as possible.
"We're closing the doors just as soon as this gentleman leaves,"
she said, pointing to me. "I'm not going anywhere," I said.
"Well, you can stay here if you want," she said, "but I'm not
dying for this godforsaken place." She hurried out the door
with the fire marshall and the last few customers
and employees. The restaurant became eerily quiet and the lights
flickered then went out completely. It sounded like
a freight train the size of Vermont was passing through town.
Then a moped blew through a nearby window and landed
in a booth followed by a heavy, gusty rain. I fell to one knee
and wiped blood and bits of glass from my hair. Then
I walked closer to the broken window and watched the tornado
approach. I closed my eyes and felt the drops of rain
on my face, listening to tires screech and people scream.
Then I heard the restaurant's entry bell and when I turned
around, there stood a beautiful woman dressed in a red evening
gown, her hair unblemished by the torrential winds. She saw me
standing by the window as a traffic light collapsed into the street
and a man was impaled by a flagpole. "Christopher?" she said,
offering me a lacy, white handkerchief. "Yes," I said. "I just
knew you'd come."

The Dead Man

    While I was mowing my lawn one afternoon, I noticed a dead man meandering down the road. He stopped in front of each house lifting his frangible skull with considerable effort, squinting the chalky pockets of his eyes, until he crumbled to his knees at the foot of my driveway and began to bawl. I didn't really know what to say, seeing as this was my first encounter with a dead man. It was nothing like I imagined it would be. He looked so alive in his sorrow. Finally, I said, "Is something the matter?" "No, no," he said reattaching his unhinged jaw. "It's just that I used to live here." "Must have been a while ago," I said. "A very long time ago," he said. "Maybe a hundred years ago." "Wow," I said. "What brings you back this way?" "Oh, I was just in the neighborhood," he said. "I thought the dead usually come out after dark," I said. He began dusting himself off. "We don't really keep a schedule," he said. "I beg your pardon," I said. "You know, it's funny," he said, gazing up at the house. "It's funny how something can look so different, yet so incredibly familiar." "I think I know what you mean," I said. "I visited the home of my late grandparents last year and it was remarkable seeing how my memories occupied the space and simultaneously, the house rejected my memories." After a moment he sighed and said, "Well, I better be heading on." "Wait," I said. "Would you like to come inside?" He hesitated and then said, "Would it be alright?" "It would be my pleasure," I said. "Please, this way." I linked my arm with his and helped him up the driveway and inside the house. When we walked through the door, he smiled and placed his disintegrating fingertips on the newel post. "I can't tell you how many times I watched my children run up and down these stairs, how many times my wife and I danced in this hallway." "Must have been very different then," I said. "Different colors sure, decorations, but otherwise it's still the same. It's got good bones, unlike these ratty old things," he said, brushing off his hollow frame. I showed him around the rest of the house and when we returned to the kitchen I said, "Would you like a cup of coffee?" "Coffee?" he said, "I haven't had coffee in decades." "I can make some, it's no problem." "If it's no trouble," he said, "that would be lovely." I made some coffee and offered him a biscotti and we sat on the back patio. He told me all about his life, what he used to do, who he used to be. Then my wife Marcia came home from work. "Raymond?" she said, "Would you mind helping me with something really quick?" "Sure," I said. "I'll be right back," I said to the dead man. "Help yourself to more coffee and biscotti." When I got inside Marcia was livid. "What's that dead man doing on our patio?" she said. "He's having coffee," I said. "Why is he having coffee?" she said. "It's okay," I said, "he used to live here."

The Little Guy

My wife and I decided to take the little guy out
for a pancake breakfast, but as soon as we walked
through the door of the restaurant the assistant manager
stormed up to us, waving her finger in the air. "You can't
bring that wild animal in here," she said. "It's a violation
of health codes and besides that, it's incredibly dangerous."
A man leaving the bathroom saw us and hid behind the dessert
carousel. At the register, a young woman fainted. Ginny and I
looked at each other and then at the assistant manager. "I know
we're not your usual clientele." I said. Then Ginny interrupted,
"But my husband and I were excited to take the little guy out
for a pancake breakfast, and come hellfire or holy water,
I demand that you seat us immediately." I was proud of her.
She always said everything I was thinking but without
hesitation. "Ruby," said the assistant manager, handing three
menus to a pimply-faced girl with braces. "Table of three."
"Who's up next?" asked Ruby. "Give them to Laverne, she'll know
what to do." As Ruby walked us through the restaurant,
I could hear the other customers gasping and wincing,
many avoiding eye contact. Ruby seated us in a far corner,
handed us our menus, and after a few minutes she sent over our
waitress, Laverne. She stopped about six feet from the table
and said, "What can I get you to drink?" "Coffees for us,"
said Ginny. "And apple juice for the little guy," I said.
"And do you all know what you'd like to eat?" "We're all going
to have the pancake breakfast," said Ginny. "Even the little
guy?" said Laverne. "Oh yes," I said. "*Especially* the little
guy." Ginny began handing Laverne our menus when she turned
her back and rushed off. "Rude," said Ginny. "Maybe she didn't
see you," I said. "Herman, everyone in this dump has been rude
to us since we arrived." "I know," I said. "Maybe we shouldn't
have come." "And let another one of these bastards win?"
said Ginny, "I don't think so." Laverne returned with our drinks
and as she got within six feet of the table, she pulled
an airhorn out from her apron pocket and blasted it in the direction

of the little guy. "Argh!" she screamed. "Get back! Get back!" Then she placed our drinks down in front of us. She blasted the airhorn again as she backed away from the table, never once taking her eyes off of us. When she reached the wait station, she said that our pancake breakfast would be right up. "That was a little unusual," I said. "More than unusual," said Ginny. "I can't believe the little guy's not bawling." "He's a pretty tough little guy," I said. "He sure is," she said. "Just like his mommy." "And his daddy," I said. "More like his mommy," said Ginny. "A bit of his daddy," I said. "Jesus, Herman," said Ginny, "give it a rest." We sat there quietly sipping our drinks and then we heard sirens getting louder and louder until they stopped just outside the restaurant. "What do you suppose is going on?" I said. "I'm really not sure," said Ginny. Several fireman and police officers came rushing in and the manager directed them toward our table. "Here we go again," said Ginny. Then I noticed Laverne charging the table with her airhorn and several pounds of ground beef. The police assembled behind her with their weapons drawn, and even the firemen had axes at the ready. Laverne fired the ground beef into the back corner of our booth and repeatedly blared her airhorn, all while shouting, "Get out, get out, get out you, you mangy motherfucker!" The firemen dragged Ginny and me out of the booth while the police officers cast nets and shot tranquilizer darts at the little guy. We listened to him snarling and resisting them. "Damn," said one of the officers. "The little guy bit me." The paramedics arrived and had surrounded us as we lay on the floor. "Okay, sir, you've lost a lot of blood. You're probably really delirious, but don't worry. We're here to help." Someone lifted my head to put an oxygen mask on me and I noticed that I was missing much of my left arm and my clothes were shredded to pieces. I looked over at Ginny, but there was no Ginny, just a pile of bones. "You're really lucky to be alive," said one of the paramedics. "One more night with little guy and you might no longer be with us."

The Kirkland Bird Club

Every other weekend I meet up with a few other retirees at the Kirkland Bird Club on 28th Street. We used to go out on the trails, but after Bernie's accident we just sat around a table in the dark, taking turns making bird calls while the others guessed. I was doing my best pileated woodpecker when there was a knock on the lodge door. We all looked at each other and then Albert started counting. "One, two, three, four, five, six, seven, we're all here. Who could that be?" "Christ, Albert, how the hell should we know, you birdbrain. Why don't you ruffle your feathers for once and check it out?" "Sheesh, Murray, you don't have to be so harsh." "It's okay, Albert," I said. "I'll go with you." "Bring another round on your way in," said Jasper. Albert and I walked to the door. The person on the other side started pounding and shouting. "Hold your house finches," I said. "We're coming." I opened the door and there stood a skinny rail of a man shaking and looking up at the sky. "What seems to be the problem?" I said. "He's shaking," said Albert. "No shit, Albert." "But it's summertime." "Go get the beers, Albert, and stop being so damn dense." I turned to the shaking man. "How can I help you, sir?" I said. The man stammered. "You, you, you guys should really get a load of this," he said. "What are you talking about?" I said. "This is the Kirkland Bird Club, isn't it?" he said. "What's left of it," I said. "I heard you guys were the greatest bird authorities this side of Oklahoma." "We were," I said. "Until everyone decided to get old and go the way of the dodo." "Oh, no," said the man. "That's really too bad." "Why is that?" I said. "Here's the beer," said Albert. "One for me," I said. "And one for our new friend." "Oh, thank you, but I shouldn't," he said, looking up into the sky. I, too, looked up into the sky. "Won't you come inside?" I said. I guided him inside the lodge and into our boardroom. "Robin?" said Morty. "No, you idiot, a grosbeak," said Frank. "Gentleman, we have a visitor, a Mister.... umm," I said. "Springer," he said. "Mr. Springer." "How can we help you, Mr. Springer?" said Frank. "It's not just me you can help," said Mr. Springer, sipping his beer. "The whole community, the whole world needs you." "What's this cuckoo talking about?" said Reggie. "There's an unusual sound in the sky, a bird," said Mr. Springer. "And what do you want us to do about it?" said Cliff. "You're supposed to be the best," said Mr. Springer. "Maybe so," said Frank, "but what do you expect us to do?" "Simple," said Mr. Springer. "Identify the call." "And why should we help you, the community, and the world?" said Reggie. "It's your calling," said Mr. Springer. "And what's in it for us?" said Cliff. "Whatever you desire," said Mr. Springer. "Fame, fortune, women, you name it." We looked at each other around the table in silence and then Albert spoke up. "Let's do it," he said. "I'm ready to spread my wings and fly like an eagle." The seven of us got up and followed Mr. Springer outside. He guided us out into the park. "Where is everybody?" I said. "Everyone's in hiding," said Mr. Springer. "How the hell long were we down there in the lodge?" said Morty. "Too long," I said. "What are we supposed to do now?" said Reggie. "Spread out and wait," said Mr. Springer. We did as he said. Then we heard a raucous caw in the sky and a trio of birds the size of airplanes circled us. They began darting down into the park as we dove into bushes and out of sight. Frank took his chances on an old telephone booth thirty yards away. One of the birds saw him, swooped down and snatched him up in its beak. "Whoa, did you guys see that? Frank just got carried away by a pterodactyl," said Cliff from behind a shrub. "No, you dickcissel, that was a quetzalcoatlus," said Albert. "Get with it."

The Honeybee

I was trimming the hedges when a honeybee stung my hand.
"Ouch," I said. "That hurt." "I beg your pardon," said the honeybee.
"That was rather witless and impulsive, wasn't it?" he said.
"What happens now?" I said, rubbing my swollen hand.
"Unfortunately, for me," said the honeybee. "I die. But before I do,
I need to ask you a small favor." "What kind of favor?" I said.
"I need you to find my wife and children and tell them what happened
to me, that I've moved on to that big honeycomb in the sky ," said the honeybee.
"Why should I?" I said. "You're the one who stung me. Why should I
do you any favors?" "Don't be cross," said the honeybee. "It's just
the sort of thing one species does for another. I'd do it for you." I thought
about it for a moment and even though I was still angry that he'd stung me,
I said, "Alright, tell me your name." "My name is Xavier Blumenthal,"
said the honeybee. "Xavier Blumenthal?" I said. "That's correct," said the
honeybee, "Xavier Blumenthal." I was about to ask him where I could find his
family, but he died right there on the spot. His delicate wings curled around his
body and his little legs went stiff. For a while I sat there in the grass thinking about
Xavier Blumenthal, about how I'd been stung at least a dozen times in my life and
not once before had the bee spoken to me. *Maybe I'm crazy*, I thought.
But I didn't feel crazy. So, I headed inside, cleaned up, and packed a rucksack
with some food, water, an extra pair of socks, a sweater, and a few other
essentials and started out on foot. I began in my front yard by the hedge
where I had been stung. I called out, first at a whisper, then more loudly,
"I'm looking for the family of Xavier Blumenthal. Does anyone know
Xavier Blumenthal?" Not so much as a fly responded. Hesitantly, I dug
into the hedge where I'd been stung. "Mrs. Blumenthal?" I said.
There came no reply from the hedge. I removed a magnifying glass
from my pack and began inspecting the trim by the driveway,
then the entire perimeter of my lawn. I even got out the ladder and climbed up
on the house. After hours of searching for any friends or family of Xavier
Blumenthal, I had yet to discover anyone. Then I remembered that honeybees
travel an average of one mile from their hive, so I double-knotted my shoes
and walked down the road. I stopped by every house along the way explaining
what had happened to me, asking if they'd ever met Xavier Blumenthal or any of
his relations, and conveying how important it was that I kept my word to him.

Every able-bodied person I spoke to, man, woman, and child, decided to join the search without hesitation. After a few hours and many miles traveled there were hundreds of us shouting, "We're looking for any relation of Xavier Blumenthal! If you're out there, please let yourself be known!" Many people brought flashlights and magnifying glasses. They were crawling on the ground, climbing trees. Some disguised themselves as bees. A few had even taken to lying very still in beds of wildflowers. Someone brought a megaphone and began buzzing into it and encouraging others to buzz as well. Whether it helped or not I don't know, but it sure boosted morale. It became quite a celebration. A young boy ambled by with a boombox on his shoulder, followed by a group of teenagers who were singing along and holding hands. Little girls and boys played with sparklers. A few guys set up a barbecue stand and sold the best ribs I've ever had in my life. After a while the fireflies came out and everyone began to get really hopeful. "Ask the fireflies," someone said. "Does anyone speak firefly?" said another. "Surely the fireflies have the answer," said an old woman. Everyone started chasing the fireflies and trying to catch them. "Be careful," I said. "You don't want to hurt them. One injured firefly will set us back a hundred years." A smiling young woman looked up at me. "It's really amazing what you've done here, bringing everyone together like this. You just might have saved us all," she said.

The State Fair

It was the last day of the state fair, approaching closing time, and I had been watching the Ferris wheel go around and around for what felt like hours. I started to feel woozy and sat down on a bench by the Tilt-a-Whirl. When I opened my eyes, I noticed the reflection of a lady in white dancing in one of the puddles from when it had rained earlier in the day. She was so graceful in her thin, lacy gown, it was like watching a ballet. I stood and looked around to find her, figuring she was performing by the elephant ear stand, or the ring toss, but she was nowhere in sight. I returned my gaze to the puddle and she danced even more whimsically than before. Again, I looked up, first at the carousel, then to the penny pitch, and even the lollipop tree, but I couldn't find her. When I looked back into the puddle, she was slowly lifting her arms and spinning so that her white gown flourished with every twist and turn. Her long, luscious legs pointed into the earth like arrows. "Does anyone else see this?" I said aloud. "Shut up, old man," said a teenager throwing popcorn at me. "But where does she come from?" I said. "Ur-AY-nus," said another adolescent, high-fiving his friends. No one around me seemed to notice anything unusual. "Everyone needs to see this," I said to a few families passing by. "It's so beautiful." "Leave us alone," a man said. "You're scaring the children," said a young mother. After a few minutes of watching the lady in white dancing in the puddle at my feet, she paused and blew me a kiss. "Are you for real?" I asked. She looked me right in the eye and smiled. "What's your name?" I said. She placed one hand on her hip, wagged her finger, and silently giggled. "Can you even hear me?" I said. Then she gestured with her index finger for me to come closer. I hesitated at first, looking around at all the passersby, but then I got down on my hands and knees and pressed my ear against the puddle. I heard what sounded like a river, and beyond that, glasses clinking together, men and women's voices and their resounding laughter. I lifted my dripping ear and looked back into the rippling puddle. The lady in white gestured once more, beckoning me to come even closer. This time I rested my head into the puddle, feeling the water soak more completely into my face and clothing. I thought, for a moment, that I felt her lips on my cheek and heard her whisper something in my ear. Then a policeman tapped my shoulder and I shot up onto my hands and knees, my face encrusted with sediment and rainwater. The lady in white laughed and blushed. The fairgrounds were completely empty other than a few homeless wanderers. "It's closing time, mister," said the officer. "I understand," I said to the officer. "But you see, she's just asked me to dance," I said, gesturing to the puddle, "and I've traveled such a long, long way."

The Attic

      I decided to move my desk into the attic. I used to write at the dining room table, but Charlotte was always hosting dinner parties and it became impossible to concentrate. The television constantly played in the living room. The kitchen was a mess. And when I worked in the bedroom, Charlotte often insisted on making love and spooning all night. The attic was the only space that I could truly limit the otherwise constant interruptions. I slept most of the day and I worked on my masterpiece at night. Occasionally, I came down from the attic to get a glass of water or something to eat. Sometimes the furniture had been rearranged or there was a new painting on the wall. One night when I was hammering away on the typewriter, I thought about lying down with Charlotte in our bed and feeling her warmth. I couldn't remember the last time I spoke to anyone, ate at a restaurant, or even went outside. Every now and then I thought about resuming normal life with Charlotte, but then I'd remember the demands of my manuscript and I knew that it was all I could manage. While I slept at my desk, the attic door would periodically open and something would be removed; a coat, a pair of boots, an umbrella, holiday decorations. Then darkness resumed and I'd drift more completely into dreams. Charlotte left food and water on my desk while I slept. She'd been doing it for so long that I no longer remembered how to take care of myself. In fact, I couldn't recall the last time I even left the attic other than to use the toilet. After a while I started hearing another man's voice and noticed wine glasses left out at night, framed photographs hanging on the walls, new toiletries in the bathroom, the scent of cologne on coats hung in the closet. At first it bothered me, imagining Charlotte with another man, but the manuscript beckoned me and I ignored her infidelity. Years went by and my desk and I crept deeper into the attic. One night I heard her arguing with someone. "It can't go on forever," he said. "You have to be more compassionate," she said. These arguments continued and Charlotte always insisted on his sympathy. Over time, the arguments ceased and gave way to smaller coats and boots in the attic, storage boxes, younger voices crying and laughing, various toys and sporting goods

inhabiting my space. One night after everyone was asleep, I came down
from the attic and saw the photographs of Charlotte, her new
husband, and their many children on the walls,
how Charlotte had aged, how the house had
changed. I could still remember the night we met.
I was sitting at a town bar and she approached me and said,
"You're not from around here, I can tell." "How can you tell?"
I said. "Well, for one," she said, "this is a small town
and I've never seen you before." "And two?" I said.
"And two," she said, "you're dressed like an aquanaut
and there isn't a body of water for more than a hundred miles."

The American Bison

I made an appointment to see a dermatologist because I couldn't seem to get a handle on my itchy scalp. "Good morning, Francis, I'm Dr. Fletcher." "It's nice to meet you," I said. "So, what brings you in today?" he said. "It's my scalp," I said. "No matter what I do, it won't stop itching." "I'm sorry to hear you're having trouble," he said, washing his hands. "I've tried a slew of dandruff shampoos, tea tree and coconut oil, apple cider vinegar, omega-3s, and baking soda," I said. "Those are all reasonable remedies," he said, "but they're not always reliable." "I couldn't focus at work anymore, so I took a leave of absence." "Better safe than sorry," he said, opening a drawer and removing a binocular loupe. "My girlfriend, Peggy, broke up with me because she said my itching was getting in the way of our sex life. I even went vegetarian in hopes that would do something, but nothing works and I'm going crazy." "It's okay, Francis, you're not broken, you're just injured. We're going to figure this one out together," he said, placing his hand on my shoulder. "Thank you, Dr. Fletcher," I said. "Don't thank me yet," he said, snickering. "Now bend your head forward please." He turned on his dermatoscope and straightened his binocular loupe. "Let's take a look, shall we?" he said. He was very gentle, parting my hair, carefully probing my scalp. "There's definitely something going on here," he said. "Do you mind if I take a skin sample?" "Will it hurt?" I said. "Only a little," he said. "But it might be our best chance to figure out what's going on." I thought for a moment, and then I said, "Okay, do it." Dr. Fletcher took out a scalpel and removed a thin layer of skin along my part. He placed it on a slide and brought it to his microscope. After a few minutes he said, "Hmm. Very interesting." "How bad is it, Doc? How bad is my dandruff?" I said. "On the bright side," he said. "It's not dandruff." "That's a relief," I said. "It's not head lice, psoriasis, or tinea capitis." "So, what is it then?" I said. "Well, I'm no expert on the subject," he said, "but it appears to be mating season." "Is that some kind of medical jargon?" I said. "Far from it," he said. "You've heard of the American bison, I assume." "Sure," I said. "They live in grassland preserves, don't they?" "That's my understanding," said Dr. Fletcher, scratching his head. "What does the American bison have to do with me?" I said. "Well, it appears that you've contracted a microscopic version of the American bison." "What are you talking about?" I said. "It's not all that uncommon. I had a guy in here last week, a really hairy fellow, complaining of body hair complications. He thought he had ingrown hairs, pimples, that sort of thing. Turns out his chest hair was just completely infested with microscopic gorillas. Hell, just yesterday I had a woman in here with a severe case of genital kangaroos." "That's unbelievable," I said. "Almost, but not quite," he said. "All that itching you're experiencing is subject to bison bulls wallowing in the dirt on your scalp. See, during a rut, when they're fighting for breeding rights, they begin by dusting up dirt for conflict. Then they bash their horns together and wrestle each other into submission. Whoever wins gets mating rights with the cow." "That's all very interesting," I said. "But what am I supposed to do? I can't live like this forever." "Hold on, hold on," said Dr. Fletcher. "Let's not get all worked up here. What is it, it's July 12th?" "Umm, yes," I said, checking my phone. "Okay, great," said Dr. Fletcher. "All that fighting and subsequent mating usually subsides around September." "What do I do until then?" I said. "The way I see it, you have two choices." "What's the first?" I said. "It's a bit radical," said Dr. Fletcher. "You either slash and burn your scalp, decimating the population, which may very well have side effects we can't even begin to imagine." "Or?" I said. "Or, and this is my personal recommendation, you can pray for an early winter with plenty of freezing temperatures and the harshest of winds." "Will that work?" I said. Dr. Fletcher assured me, "As long as you avoid wearing a hat, they should eventually migrate onto another scalp before too long."

The Unicorn

Margot and I were out for a walk in the neighborhood when we saw an elderly man slumped over in Mrs. Sullivan's prized petunias. He was dressed in all white and wore a conical hat on his forehead. "Are you alright, mister?" said Margot. "Are you hurt?" I said. "You don't know the struggles," he said. "I was just helping myself to some of these lovely petunias," he said, wiping the remains of petals from his lips. "Those are Mrs. Sullivan's prized petunias," said Margot. "They certainly are delicious," he said. "What happened to you?" I said. "I was just strolling along, minding my own business when Mrs. Cornwell's chocolate lab attacked me and I collapsed into these tasty perennials." "Oh, dear," said Margot. "And Mrs. Cornwell just left you here?" "Worse," he said. "She straddled me and tried removing my horn." "Why would she do that?" I said. "I think she's trying to live forever," he said. "What a bitch," I said. "*Daniel*," said Margot. "No, he's right," said the man. "She's up to no good. I heard her muttering something about returning with a pair of shears." "We better get you out of here," I said. "It's no use," he said. "I can't take another step." "Surely there's something we can do," said Margot. "We can't just leave you like this," I said. "There's nothing you can do for me now," he said, lifting his hat to show us his bloody wound. "Oh no," I said, looking down the road. "There's Mrs. Cornwell. She's only two blocks away." "Thank God she has a bad hip," said Margot. "That'll buy us some time." "That's the spirit," I said. "Hurry," said the man. "We don't have a moment to waste. Now listen closely. I want you to take my horn." "Why us?" I said. "I guess I have a weakness for the pure of heart and spirit," he said, winking at me. "Now take it," he said, carefully stretching the elastic strap and handing us the conical hat. "All you have to do is wear it and make a wish. Now go." "We can't leave you," said Margot. She began to cry and held his hand. "You have to," he said. "And without the power of my horn I'll be gone before she even reaches me." "We have to go," I said. "I'll never forget you," said Margot. "I know," said the man. Then Margot and I looked at each other like spooked zebras on the edge of the desert. We knew the only way to survive was to camouflage, so we rounded the corner and ducked into what appeared to be an underwear protest. Thousands of people had gathered in their underwear and were shouting things like "*Everyone *wants the wingspan of the wandering albatross, but is never willing to do the work!*" and, "*I could never juggle a handful of cherry bombs that does not lead to plot!*" Margot and I quickly stripped down to our underwear. She tucked the conical hat into her white bra and shouted, "*Every one of us is reaching for barely visible mists of epiphany!*" The crowd applauded and cheered and tightened around her. Then Margot waved to me, carefully stretched the elastic band of the conical hat, placed it on her forehead, and shouted, "*It's been so long since I confessed to being born on the cracked side of a leaking snow globe!*" I tried reaching for her, but I was thrust backward by the crowd. "*I am doubtless a fool,*" I called out, "*a strategic double negative advancing slowly into the trembling earth!*" No one seemed to hear me, so I shouted, "*All I know is the ringing of a telephone, the blowing of the wind, an infant screaming in its crib renouncing all limits of a musical coda!*" But it was too late. Margot disappeared into the camouflage of protesters and I never saw her again.

Santa Claus

"It's no use," said Mildred. "I can't eat." She carelessly dropped her fork against her plate and began to weep. "Pass the asparagus, would you please," I said. Mildred wiped her cheeks with her napkin and passed the asparagus. "This is a wonderful dinner," I said, lifting a turkey leg to my lips. "You really should have some." "I don't know how you can eat at a time like this," said Mildred. "It's not like anybody died," I said, scooping a heap of mashed potatoes out of the bowl and slapping them down onto my plate. "Yet," said Mildred. "What?" I said. "Yet," said Mildred. "Nobody has died *yet*." "Salt and pepper, please," I said, rolling my eyes. "Don't look at me like that," said Mildred. "Like what?" I said. "You're making light of the situation," said Mildred. "Why shouldn't I?" I said. "You take everything so seriously all the time, it's a marvel you even know how to laugh." "Oh, Bert, that's not fair," said Mildred. "I mean, I can't believe you canceled the New Year's party," I said. "We couldn't have our friends over here, not with that *thing* in the corner," said Mildred, pointing to Santa Claus, who farted in his sleep beneath our browning Christmas tree. "Are you kidding?" I said. "He would have stolen the show." "Look at him," said Mildred. "That's not a sight worth celebrating." His belt was missing and his red and white wool coat had fallen open to reveal an engorged, pasty white belly. "Maybe not at the moment," I said. "But slip him a few whiskies and just imagine the possibilities." "I don't want to imagine the possibilities, Bert, I want him out of our living room and out of our house." "Come on," I said. "It's like he said, he merely needs a little while to cool down after the holidays and he just happened to like it here." "But Bert," said Mildred, "the way he *looks* at me, especially after a few whiskies." "What do you mean?" I said. "He just gives me the willies," said Mildred. "Yesterday he asked me to sit on his lap, and well…" "Well, what?" I said. "I think he was enjoying it a little too much." "Of course, he was, he's Santa Claus." "No," said Mildred, "he told me that Mrs. Claus never visits the 'South Pole' anymore, and then he winked at me." A few hours later, Mildred and I were watching the ball drop ceremony when we heard a voice outside coming through a megaphone. "We know you're in there, Claus, come out with your hands up." Mildred and I rushed to the window where a huge searchlight shined directly into our living room and a SWAT team took position around

the perimeter of our house. Just then, Santa Claus sprang up from underneath
our Christmas tree, guzzled some whiskey, smashed a window
by the buffet with his elbow and shouted, "You'll never take me alive,
you sons of bitches!" It was then he bent down and quickly rifled
through his sack. He pulled out a tommy gun and began firing
at the officers. He killed two and injured a few others
before they even started firing back. When they did, Mildred and I
dove down on the carpet as shots poured through our house,
blowing apart our picture window, many of our framed photos
and the baby grand. Mildred and I crawled to each other
as the New Year's Eve countdown had begun. *Ten, nine.*
Santa pulled the clip out of a grenade and killed half a dozen
troopers approaching from the east. *Eight, seven.* "I'm sorry
for everything, Mildred," I said. "I should've listened to you
from the beginning." *Six, five.* "No," said, Mildred, "You were
right, this would have been the party of the century." *Four, three.*
We could hear the bell-adorned reindeer on the roof
dropping like flies. *Two, one.* A series of shots shattered our television
to pieces. At last, Santa was clipped in the neck and began bleeding
out on the floor. "Happy New Year, my love," said Mildred. "Happy
New Year," I said, leaning in for a kiss.

Lucky Penny

"Here, let me get that for you!" I said, pulling out Penny's chair. "That's very kind," she said as I scooted her forward. "It's nice to see that chivalry isn't as dead as they say it is." "My mother taught me well," I said, sitting down and looking at Penny across the candlelit table. "This is a lovely restaurant," said Penny. "I've always wanted to come here." "Yeah, me too, I'm really happy we decided to get together," I said, placing my napkin in my lap. "It's so hard to meet people nowadays." "I know," she said, "I'm happy too. I almost gave up hope that anyone decent was actually left." "And who knows," I said, "maybe you'll turn out to be my lucky Penny." "We'll see," said Penny, smiling. "Only time will tell." "In all sincerity," I said, "you seem like a really genuine person, and I think we have a lot in common. It doesn't hurt that you're incredibly beautiful, either." "You're one to talk," said Penny. "Not to sound weird or anything, but I'm just so glad you actually look like your profile picture." "Is that unusual?" I said. "You'd be surprised," said Penny. The waiter came over and we ordered drinks and an appetizer. While we waited for him to return, Penny said, "Listen, I don't really date that much." "That's okay," I said. "I don't either." "I just hate all the nervous small talk that goes into it, you know? Like, do I have enough in common with this person to see them again? Do I want to sleep with them? Do I need an escape plan?" Penny said, laughing. "Yeah, I know what you mean," I said. "I get tired of the interview and wondering whether I'm answering questions honestly or just going through the motions." The waiter placed our drinks in front of us. We each took a couple long sips and looked around the room. "I have an idea," said Penny. "What's that?" I said. "What do you say we skip the first date?" Penny said. "Yikes, that was a fast rejection," I said. "No, no, that's not what I mean," Penny said, touching my hand. "What I mean is, like, maybe we can skip to the highlights and then just fill in the blanks as we go. Pretend we've been doing this for a while." "Like how long?" I said, leaning in. "Well," said Penny, "what would you do right now if we had been seeing each other for, say, three months already?" "Three months," I said. "Hmm, well, if that were the case then I'd really like you to meet my mother." Penny sipped her drink and thought for a moment.

"Sure, I'd like to meet your mother." "Great," I said, pulling a glass tube filled with ashes from my pocket. "This is Mother. Well, part of her at least. Which part, I don't know." Penny looked at the glass tube and then at me, her eyes glistening with tears. "She's beautiful," said Penny. "Which part of her do you think it is?" "I like to think that it's her eyes, maybe her heart," I said. "That's lovely," she said. "I'd like to think that I have my father's smile." "Mother, this is Penny." I held up the glass tube so that Mother could get a good look at Penny. "It's nice to meet you, Mother," said Penny. "You have a very kind and handsome son." "You can hold her if you want," I said. "She won't mind." Penny held Mother in her hands and I could feel myself falling for her as I watched how delicately she handled the glass tube, how she held it to her ear as if to listen. "Oh," said Penny, "your mother would get along so well with my father. I wish I'd thought to bring him. You just never know what kind of date it's going to be." "That's okay," I said. "Maybe you could come over after dinner?" she said. "We could have a nightcap, and we could introduce them." "I'd like that," I said. From then on Mother and Father went everywhere with us. Penny loved Mother dearly, as if she were her own mother. She'd jokingly say things like, "Is that your mother in your pocket or are you just happy to see me?" Sometimes it was Mother, but usually I was happy to see her. And Father and I got along really well, for a couple of stubborn introverts. After a few months of dating, it felt as if we'd been together for years. We moved in together and quite naturally, what was mine became hers and what was hers became mine, and our lives became indistinguishable from each other. At some point in time, even Mother and Father's ashes got mixed together. We didn't think anything of it at first, but eventually things between Penny and me started getting weird. "I just don't feel comfortable now that our parents are together," said Penny. "When I kiss you, it feels like I'm kissing my brother." We tried our best to suppress those familial urges, but it was no use. Then one night we went to a party and without thinking anything of it, I introduced Penny as my sister. She put her head on my shoulder and patted my belly, and then went on a long tangent about our childhood together. "He was so adorable," she said. "And he had the funniest way of saying 'sister'."

The Rooster

Edwin knocked on my office door, leaned in, and said, "Some of the boys and I are heading out for drinks, are you in?" "Whoa, where did you get that hat?" I said. "Oh, you like it?" he said. "It's a game changer," I said. "Thanks," he said, "I think so, too." "I've been thinking about picking up a new hat, myself." "Well then, you've got to check out Lorenzo's on Tenth Street," said Edwin. "It'll be the last hat you ever need to buy." "Oh yeah?" I said. "Yeah man, it's a magical experience. I mean I've never really been a hat guy, but something about that place changed my life." "That's amazing," I said. "Truly. The only thing is..." said Edwin, averting his eyes. "What?" I said. "Be prepared," Edwin said. "For what?" I said. "There are certain conditions," said Edwin. "What do you mean, *conditions*?" "Well, you see, he chooses your hat," said Edwin. "Who?" I said. "Lorenzo," Edwin said. "He's very good, been doing it for years, but he's very particular." "So, I can't go in there, look around, and buy any hat I want?" "No," said Edwin. "It's not that kind of place. That's the beauty of it. When you walk in, he leads you to the middle of the room where there's a chair. He'll have you sit down and then he'll ask you one question." "What's the question?" "Supposedly it's a different question for every customer," said Edwin. "What did he ask you?" I said. "He asked me...aw, Christ it sounds so ridiculous outside of the shop," said Edwin. "Tell me," I said. Edwin sighed. "He asked me what I would do if I were the ruler of an underwater world." "What did you say?" I said. "Well, that's the crazy part, I didn't say anything," he said. "You don't say anything, you just think it, and then based on your thoughts he fits you for a hat. I don't know how he does it." "That sounds insane," I said. "Maybe, but I'd never have picked this out for myself," said Edwin, sliding his finger along the brim. "And look at me now! I've never been more confident." "Yeah, that is something," I said, tapping my pencil on my desk. "Something extraordinary." "Anyway, man, you coming?" said Edwin. "Actually," I said. "I think I'll check out Lorenzo's and see what it's all about." "You won't regret it," said Edwin. "Call me later and let me know how it goes." I grabbed my coat and walked east. After a few blocks I was standing outside Lorenzo's. As I approached, a man opened the door for a woman dabbing her eyes with a handkerchief. "Thank you," she said. "I always wondered what life would be like if dogs took over the world." "You're welcome, Mrs. Napier. Come back any time." She blew her nose into her handkerchief and slowly walked down the road, holding her new hat fast to her head as the wind picked up. I looked back at the storefront and the gentleman was still holding the door. "It's alright," he said. He motioned me forward. "I've known Mrs. Napier for many years," he said. "She's always had a very deep, emotional connection to her hats." He patted my shoulder and led me inside. "How can I help you?" he said. "A guy I work with, uh, Edwin Palmer, recommended I stop by." "Yes, Edwin," he said. "He was complicated, but I figured him out." "You must be Lorenzo," I said. "Yes," he said, "and these are my hats." "I've never seen so many hats in one place," I said. "I mean, I've been to hat shops before, but nothing like this." "Yes," said Lorenzo. "So, I imagine that if you spoke to Mr. Palmer then you understand how this works." "Yes," I said. "And I only accept cash," he said. "That's fine," I said. "This way, then," he said. Lorenzo led me toward an old oak chair in the middle of the room. "Please, take off your coat and sit down," he said. "Now close your eyes," he said. "Alright," I said. "I want to tell you a story," he said. "I thought you asked a question," I said. "I'm going to tell you a story first," he said. "Alright," I said. "There's no reason to believe that the duck," he said, "who migrates hundreds of miles every spring and fall at an altitude of 4,000 feet, had anything to gain from piloting a sky-blue silk balloon as spectators gasped and applauded its ascent. The sheep, on the other hand, whose hooves had only lifted to trot across a grassy field by two, maybe three inches at a time depending on its intent, would have been heralded for his preternatural flight. It was the rooster who completed their trinity, the rooster who normally journeys a mere six feet off the ground to escape a predator or to command the attention of a reticent hen. As they set aloft that glorious autumn day in 1783 assisted by light winds carrying them two miles during the longest eight minutes of their lives, it was long enough for the duck to sleep, long enough for the sheep to consider his immortality, and long enough, still, for the cock to reveal his dastardly plan of escape as they sailed uncontrollably in a waxen sky, climbing higher and higher toward the sun in a balloon heated by burning straw and wool." Lorenzo paused and cleared his throat. "My question for you sir: Are you the duck, the rooster, or the sheep?" "What kind of question is that?" I said. Shortly after I spoke there was a hat upon my head. I felt woozy and Lorenzo helped me to my feet and into my coat. "Everything will be alright," he said. "It was always going to be this way." I buttoned my coat and looked at myself in the mirror. I felt as if there were

no ceiling at all. I paid Lorenzo for the hat and then he opened the door for me. "It was always going to be this way," he said once again, grinning sympathetically. I stepped onto the sidewalk and breathed the cold, sharp October air into my lungs. When I turned back to thank him, the police tackled me onto the ground, one placing his knee on my back while another cuffed my wrists.
"What's going on?" I said. One of the other officers radioed in, "Don't worry Chief, we got him." I had always longed to be arrested, to finally be saved.

The Village

Garfield hadn't missed a day of work in years. Then one day
he didn't show up. I didn't think much of it, but when he missed
another day, and then another, I started to worry. We weren't
particularly close, but seeing as he was my cubicle neighbor,
I decided to take a long lunch and stop by his house. I walked up
the porch steps and knocked on the door. I looked through
his windows and noticed that all the furniture had been pushed
against the wall, some pieces even stacked upon one another.
I heard what sounded like a train whistle. After another minute,
the door swung open and Garfield grabbed me by the shirt
and dragged me inside. "Don't say a word," he whispered. I fell
to the floor as he looked out the window, locked the door
and fastened the chain. "What are you doing here?" he said. He was
dressed like a train conductor and holding a shiny red whistle. He
looked as if he'd been crying. "You haven't been to work in three days,"
I said. "Does anyone else know you're here?" he said. "No, I just wanted
to check in, that's all." "Shut up," he said. "Listen." I listened to the silence.
"Do you hear it?" he said. "Hear what?" I said. "Shut up," he said.
As I listened to the unbroken calm, I noticed that the middle of the living
room floor held an entire miniature village full of townspeople laboring through
infinite stillness: mothers swept their porches for eternity; locked in mid-stride,
children pursued a stationary ball without satisfaction; men bound to the
wrecking ball of masculine labor slaved in the coal mine,
the pharmacy, the office building, the park, and the train station. The trees
defied seasonal change with effortless, verdant branches, their color
succumbing only to dust. The scintillating surface of the cellophane lake,
dependent on the life of a sixty-watt bulb, glistened with an astonishing current.
And the train, to which Garfield had turned, knelt down, and restarted, buried
the silence under its interminable roar. With profound mobility, it encircled
the entirety of civilization in a matter of seconds. "They're moving," he said.
"What's moving?" I said. "Them," he said, pointing to the village. "They're moving.
They move." I looked closely at the village to see a man eternally holding
a bucket of water, a doctor listening for a heartbeat in a waxen chest,
the farmer's daughter bending generously in her calico patterned dress
and apron to feed the chickens who, judging by their attentiveness,

seemed to know more than they were letting on. It must have been the way she smiled while dashing grain into their path that caught my eye, or the vigorous determination of the handsome farmhand pitching a loose bale of hay toward the mare peeking out of the ramshackle stable. Maybe it was the way the aging widow frustratedly beat her rug with a stick as it hung from a wavering clothesline, which only brought me closer to the celibate distance between her and her late husband's grave. I noticed how the kitchen curtains gently lifted over a cooling pie as if to portend the carnal innuendos of the wind, and how the hound flirted with his stiff tail. I lifted a stallion out of the pasture and looked closely, waiting for it to buck and neigh. "I wouldn't do that if I were you," said Garfield. "Why not?" I said. "It's like playing God." "Farmer Crowley doesn't approve of anyone handling his livestock." Then Garfield hit me over the head with a lamp and I blacked out. When I awoke, all the townspeople had gathered around me and many were upon me. They had tightly bound me with rope, emptied my pockets and tore away loose threads on my clothing. I felt the conductor's hat upon my head and the shiny, red whistle dangled from my neck. I couldn't move and I began to panic. I noticed Garfield watching through the opened window on the porch. "Garfield," I said. "Garfield, help me." "I'm sorry, James, I just couldn't stand it anymore," he said. "What's going on?" I said, as Farmer Crowley jabbed my nose with a pitchfork. "They said if I found a replacement in time for the county fair then I was free to go. All you have to do is blow into the windmill and the cranks and pulleys will operate the lights and the rides. It's a simpler time," he said. "You'll understand, someday. And when you do, you'll be the best conductor the village has ever seen." He stepped away from the window and I shouted after him. "What happens when Eleanor gets home?" I said, trying to free myself. "Who?" he said, briefly reappearing at the window. "Your wife," I said.
"What happens when Eleanor gets home?" "Eleanor?" he said.
"There is no Eleanor. Never was."

The Clicking Sound

Leah was cutting up carrots, celery, and onion for soup when she said, "What's that sound?" I listened for a moment then finished uncorking the wine. "It's a funny clicking sound," said Leah. "I don't hear anything," I said, handing her a glass of cabernet. "I swear I heard something," she said. "I really hope we don't have mice or bats or anything like that." "I'm sure it's nothing," I said. After a while the soup was simmering and we were onto another glass of wine. "That soup smells delicious," I said. "I'm so hungry I could eat a horse." "There it is again," said Leah. "What?" I said. "That sound," she said. "Have you checked the attic recently?" "I was actually just up there the other day going through some old boxes," I said. "You didn't see or hear anything?" said Leah. "I didn't," I said. "Just dust and junk." "It's probably nothing," she said. "Maybe I'm just hearing the ice machine or the heating vents turning on." "I'm sure that's all it is," I said. "And if it's something else, I'm sure Slippers will find it." That night Leah shook me out of a sound sleep. "Hank, Hank, wake up!" "What is it?" I said. "That sound," said Leah. "I think it's in the room." "Go back to sleep," I said. "Hank, *please*," said Leah. I cleared my eyes and sat up in bed. I listened closely. At first, I didn't hear anything at all, and then ever so subtly came the clicking sound from across the room. "Get your phone," I said. "Why?" said Leah. "Because I left mine in the living room," I said. "Who are you calling?" said Leah. "No one," I said. "I want to shine a light on it." "Oh, God," said Leah, "I don't want to see it." "We have to," I said. "Otherwise, we won't know what we're dealing with." "Fine," she said, handing me her phone and pulling the covers up to her eyes. I shined the light toward the corner. "Ew, gross," said Leah. "What is it?" Sitting in an antique rocker, which we had never seen before, was a very old and deformed woman crocheting a scarf. "What do I do?" I whispered. "*Get her*," said Leah. "Get her?" I said. Then the very old and deformed woman looked into the flashlight and said, "Green is the color of new beginnings,"

before clicking her needles together and rocking forward
and backward, forward and backward. Leah screamed, "Hank,
Hank, oh my God, *Hank!*" Over her screams I heard a man
yell, "CUT!" All the lights came on in our bedroom as well as a few
additional flood lights strategically positioned by the windows.
A flurry of people walked through serving coffee, handing out
notes, changing film, and primping costumes. Then the
assistant director stood up on our bed, and shouted, "Lunch
break!" and the very old and deformed woman stood up out
of her rocking chair, relieved a wedgie, tore off her wig,
and sprinted to the bathroom, mumbling, "I can't believe
this is how I'm ending my career."

The Waiting Room

In the waiting room a woman carefully lifted a bright orange bowling ball from her handbag, exposed her left breast, inserted her nipple into the thumb hole and began to hum and rock from side to side. After a few minutes she stood up pressing the bowling ball to her breast and looked at me. "I'm so sorry," she said. "I don't know what's the matter." "It's no trouble," I said. "It's not usually so finicky," she said. "It's probably just tired." "I understand," I said. "Mine's like that all the time," said a woman burping a xylophone. "That's the truth," said another woman changing the soiled diaper of a dreamcatcher. Then a man walked in pulling a red wagon behind him. He signed in at the receptionist's desk and turned around to say, "Well, if you'd gotten up when I told you to, then you would have had time for breakfast. You need to start being a better listener." He sat down and parked his wagon beside him. Rifling through a magazine, he said to the wagon, "Not another word." "Dudley," called the nurse. A woman stood up, lifted a bean bag chair over her shoulder, and said, "C'mon baby, it's our turn." She patted the chair and said, "It's going to be alright. Everything's going to be just fine." In the corner, dozens of wind-up toys flipped forward and rolled backward. Some even took off across the floor and stopped only when they hit the wall. A woman in her thirties, who looked completely harried, tried to stop them. The man next to me leaned over while bouncing a remote-controlled car on his knee and whispered, "If I ever have that many, just shoot me." "I know what you mean," I said, just to be a part of the commiseration. Then the nurse appeared again from the back and called, "Williams." I stood up from my chair and straightened the frills on the throw pillow sitting between my legs. I lifted it up and gave it a gentle pat on the rear. "They're always sweet at that age aren't they?" said a grandmother toting a furnished dollhouse inhabited by a family of five, a dog, and a cat. "Enjoy it while it lasts."

The Sky

A week after our son was born, Janice opened the curtains and suggested we bring him outside. "He's never really seen the outside before." "I don't know," I said, reluctantly. "What if something happens?" "Nothing's going to happen," she said. We walked him around the yard to show him the flower garden and the birdbath, and then we laid him in the grass to listen to the world. Our neighbors from two doors down, Marvin and Abby, slowed their car in front of our house. "Beautiful boy," Marvin said. "But I'd get him indoors soon. Storm's coming," he said, pointing to the sky. "Thank you," I said. They drove off and we both looked up to a clear azure sky. "We should probably get him inside," I said. Then Joey, our paperboy, raced by throwing newspapers haphazardly from left to right, looking up worriedly as he passed. "Relax, Ned," said Janice. "There's not a cloud in the sky." "You don't think it smells like rain?" I said. "Stop being so paranoid," said Janice. "Everything's fine. Come sit with us." "I just get so worried that something is going to happen to him." "What could possibly happen?" said Janice. I walked over and sat with them in the grass. It felt good to be a family. Andrew held my pinky finger in his hand and brought it to his lips. I kissed Janice on the forehead as she watched him flinch his little limbs. After a few minutes I said, "Did you hear that?" "What?" said Janice, tickling the baby. Then a deep, crackling sound echoed throughout the neighborhood. "Probably just thunder in the distance," said Janice. A few pedestrians stopped and looked around. Several cars crawled to a stop and drivers peered out through their open windows, some even stepping completely out of them. Then our next-door neighbor Maude dropped her hose and shouted, "The sky!" We all looked up and watched as the heavens began to split like ice on a frozen lake. It webbed out in every direction, lines of dull gray intersecting blue. It appeared to be cracking under the weight of something trying to cross

overhead. For a moment everything stabilized,
briefly silent and still, but then we watched the outline
of several footprints press down, breaking loose long
cerulean shards. "Get the baby!" I shouted. Janice
scooped him up and ran for the house. I looked around
as broad fragments impaled whole houses and little chips
rained down, flaying trees and vehicles. Everyone
screamed and ran for cover. I hurried to the porch
just as a large herd of hadrosaurs somersaulted through
the splintered empyrean, some trying to hold on
to the surface of the sky, before helplessly descending
to the ground in a heap of groaning rubble.

The Brown Bear

I was hunting grouse in Alaska when I came across a brown bear. "Don't move, or I'll shoot," I said. "Lower your weapon or I'll eat you," he said. "I don't want to be eaten," I said. "Well, I don't want to be shot," he said. "What do you suggest?" I said. "I suggest we figure out an alternative," he said. "That sounds like a mighty fine idea," I said. "After all, the sun will be setting in a little while, and it's already pretty cold." "We could go our separate ways," he said. "How do I know you won't attack me when I turn my back?" I said. "You don't," he said, "but how do I know you won't shoot me when I turn mine?" "You don't," I said. "We could camp here for the night," he said, "and talk about it over dinner?" "I can't camp here," I said. "I don't have any supplies, and besides, it's only a mile or so to my house." "Well, I think there's only one thing we can do," he said. "Seeing as I've been on my own now for a long, long time and have gotten pretty lonely, I suggest I come home with you to live out the rest of my days. That way we can be sure to keep an eye on each other." "I don't know about that," I said. "What if you kill me in my sleep?" "What if you kill me in mine?" he said. "I wouldn't do that," I said. "It's unsportsmanlike." "Sounds fair to me," he said. "I don't have a very big house," I said. "I don't need a lot of room," he said. "I could just lie down in front of your fireplace like a rug. You wouldn't even know I was there." "I don't have a rug," I said. "And those wooden floors do get pretty chilly at night." "You could even sit on my back and roast hot dogs in the fire," he said. "I do like hot dogs," I said. "It's settled then," said the brown bear. So, we walked home together side by side, sharing stories of our lives alone in the Alaskan wilderness. When we arrived at the cabin, he was true to his word. He lie down in front of the fireplace like a rug, stretching out his legs and flattening himself as best he could. I hung up my rifle over the fireplace and that night I sat on

his back and roasted hot dogs over the dashing flames. Though
he was a pretty bumpy rug, when he breathed, I felt like
I was afloat on the ocean. I was grateful he was there. And when
he died several years later, I dressed him and tossed his organs
to the wolves. Then I climbed inside of him and imagined I was
the very meal that assured his survival during an unrelenting winter.

Digging

I was in the backyard digging a grave for my dead cat when a jogger passing by nearly stumbled to the ground. "What on Earth are you doing?" she said, pressing her face against the chain link fence. "I'm digging a grave," I said, pointing to the dead cat with my shovel. "I'd strongly advise you to reconsider," she said. "I mean, I know human beings can be pretty horrible to each other, but surely there's another way." "If I don't bury her," I said, "the raccoons and other night creatures will get her. It'd be an awful mess." "It's your funeral," she said, before jogging away. Then, my neighbor Barney walked over and stopped at the property line and said, "You digging to China?" "I wasn't planning on it," I said. "What are you doing with that shovel then?" he said. "Slippers died this morning," I said. "Oh no," he said. "Slippers?" "Yeah, Slippers," I said. "Be that as it may," he said, "I wouldn't go digging a hole to China." "I wouldn't do that," I said. "It's been catching," he said, "the digging." "I hadn't heard," I said. "It's true," he said. "In fact, Diane hasn't seen Philip in nearly a week. He said he was going to dig a garden, but everyone knows he was digging to France. MaryBeth across the street has gone missing. The Jacobys said just before she vanished, she was talking about Italy and Malta. Even the Brennans! The whole family started digging earlier this month and no one has seen them since. Maybe it's nothing, or maybe it's a family vacation to the Netherlands." "That's horrible," I said. "But I'm not planning on going anywhere, just burying Slippers is all." "Just be careful," said Barney, "that's how it all gets started. One good deed and the whole world turns inside out. Welp, I'll leave you to it." "Take care," I said. I sank my shovel three feet into the soft earth and listened to it thrash and clink its face on stubborn roots and chipped rock. I couldn't help but think, at least for a moment, that it was possible if I kept digging through crust, mantle and core I might eventually reach the other side. Then, as I dragged the final inches of clay and stone from the grave with my bare hands, it occurred to me that if I were to reach the other side, I would surface at the bottom of the Indian Ocean. All that water would flush me backward to where I began, digging a grave for an old friend whose lifeless body I lifted from the ground, immediately noting the difference in her weight without breath.

The Drawbridge

I arrived home from work to find that my house was surrounded by a large moat. I parked across the street and walked to the edge of the yard. "I wouldn't get too close if I were you," said a man standing on my front porch steps. "The waters are full of man-eating alligators." He was dressed in chainmail and royal arms and he was grooming a horse. "But this is my house," I said. "I live here." "Not as of noon today," he said. "King Edward's army conquered this land to no contest late this morning. It is now officially part of the King's domain." "But I've got to feed my dog. I have bills to pay. Kelly's coming for dinner in just over an hour." "I'm afraid there's nothing I can do," he said. "You weren't here to defend your castle, so by all rights it was free for the taking." "My name is on the mortgage," I said. "And besides, I couldn't have been here. It's Wednesday and I have a job." "You could have at least posted guards at the towers and along the perimeter." "I don't have any guards," I said. "I'm not a king." "That couldn't be more obvious," he said, leading his horse into my front yard. "How did you even get inside?" I said. "Battering ram," he said. "And without archers on the rooftop or reinforcements at the gate, it was all too easy." "How did this moat get here, and the alligators?" I said. "Any fool knows there's no point in having a drawbridge if you don't have a moat," he said. "I guess you're right," I said. "What am I supposed to do now?" "You can wander about, begging, scavenging for scraps, or maybe some desperate widow will take you in." "I can't do that," I said. "There's no place for me out there. This is my home." "Well, King Edward is looking for a new jester," he said. "What happened to the last one?" I said. "He was beheaded for staring at the Queen's bosom," he said. "Are you a bosom man?" "Typically, I pride myself on being an ass man," I said. "But I've been known to linger on a bosom. Does she have a nice bosom?" I said. "Exquisite," he said. "That does boast a challenge," I said. "If you're up to it," he said, "the rewards can be quite handsome." "Lower the drawbridge," I said. "I've lived a good life."

The Instruction Manual

Zelda and I were kissing on the sofa and things were really beginning to heat up. Then I said, "I've got to be honest, I haven't gone to bed with a woman in almost three years." "Really?" she said. "Yes," I said. "I don't know if you're aware," she said, "but a lot has changed in the last three years. Some things might get lost in translation." "Surely it hasn't become all that complicated," I said. "I always thought it was pretty straightforward." "Not anymore," she said. "I was actually going to say something when you started kissing me without first showing me all the emergency exits. I figured maybe you were just a bit of a daredevil. But then you started feeling my breasts without reciting the Greek alphabet and I knew something was off." "I had no idea," I said. "No one ever talks about intimacy anymore. I didn't realize the ritual had become so complicated." "It's okay," she said, kissing me. "Do you have any dry ice, or possibly a bottle of formaldehyde?" "I don't think so," I said, scratching my head. "That's fine," she said. "We really shouldn't be getting ahead of ourselves. That's really like fourth or fifth date stuff." "Alright," I said, feeling relieved. "What about motor oil and a pinch of chewing tobacco?" she said. "Now that I can do," I said, running out of the living room and into the garage. When I returned, Zelda had unbuttoned her blouse and was lying seductively on the sofa. "Do you want to make our way to the bedroom?" I said. She sat up on the couch and began sifting through her bag. "I don't know," she said. "Have you ever operated a submarine?" She removed a large book from her bag and set it on the coffee table. "In the bathtub," I said. "You're cute," she said, sliding me the instruction manual. "I hope you're a thorough reader," she said as she handed me a highlighter and slipped out of her pants. "Some men think they know everything. But then they get down there, and sure enough, it's like catching a snowflake with a flamethrower."

A Real Family

We had just come back from a day at the beach when I went into my study to examine a new specimen I found along the dunes. I placed it in a petri dish and slid it under the microscope. I saw some movement and when I focused the lens, I realized it was a nearly-imperceptible family picnicking on the coast. The mother was lying on her back sunning herself and rubbing lotion over her body. The little girl was building a sand castle and the father and son were tossing a frisbee and laughing at the seagulls. "Mandy, get in here," I said. The family looked around as if they heard me and the mother covered up with a shawl. "What is it, Mitch? I was just unpacking," she said, placing her hands on my shoulders. "Sit down," I said. "Take a look at this." "What is it?" said Mandy. "Just look," I said. I stood up and Mandy sat in my chair to peer into the microscope. "Do you see it?" I said. "Good Lord," said Mandy. "Incredible, isn't it?" I said. "Mitch, baby, what is this?" "A sample I took from the dunes at the beach," I said. "It's crazy, isn't it?" Mandy looked closer and I paced around the room. "This is just amazing," I said. "We're going to be rich and famous and nothing is ever going to be the same." "Mitch?" said Mandy. "I wonder who I call first, the authorities? The *Times*? This is just so remarkable!" "Mitch?" said Mandy. "Mitch!" "What?" I said. "I think this woman is me," said Mandy, looking up at me. "What do you mean, she's you?" She looked back at the family. "I mean, she's me, I'm certain of it." "Let me see," I said. Mandy stood up and I sat down in the chair. "Not now me, but, like, future me." "Future you?" I said. "I'm a little older there, but it's definitely me. You can see my birthmark." "I'll be damned," I said. "And I'll tell you something else," said Mandy. "The father is you. No question." "Wow," I said. "I've put on some weight." "And those are our children," said Mandy, wrapping her arms around me. "We're parents," I said, turning around to kiss her. "A family," she said. "A real, honest-to-God family."

The Woods

We were at the lake for the weekend and Valerie suggested we go hiking through the woods. "There's supposed to be a beautiful waterfall at the end of Hawks' Nest Trail," said Valerie. "We could pack a late lunch." "That sounds great," I said. We hiked into the woods and reached the waterfall by late afternoon. "The falls are so much bigger than I expected," I said, catching my breath. "It's incredible," said Valerie. "Do you want to unpack the food?" I said. "Maybe rest a little while?" "I'm going for a swim," said Valerie. "Really?" I said. "Why not?" she said. "You should come." "We don't have any swimwear," I said. "There's no one else here," said Valerie as she took off her clothes and hung them on a tree branch. I watched her tiptoe across the pebble shore and wade into the water. "How is it?" I said. "You have to get in here," said Valerie, going under and popping back up. "It's perfect." Reluctantly, I took off my clothes and splashed in after her. "I haven't been skinny-dipping since I was a kid," I said as I swam to her. "It's invigorating, isn't it?" said Valerie. "It's like we're supposed to be this way." We swam to the waterfall and then Valerie disappeared behind it. "Valerie?" I said. "There's a little cove back here," she said, slipping out from behind the falls. We crawled onto the rocky platform and into a hidden grassy meadow surrounded by trees. "It's like another world back here," I said. "Come here," said Valerie, kissing me. We made love in the grass and quickly fell asleep under the sun. When I awoke, it was nightfall and Valerie was gone. "Valerie," I said. "Valerie, where are you?" Then a clicking sound came out of the woods and a small desk lamp turned on. "Valerie?" I said. "Valerie has been deleted," said a man in a cardigan as he rolled another page into his typewriter. "I just didn't feel like she added anything to the story."

The Rope

     Lydia and I were having a romantic dinner at the French restaurant downtown to celebrate our tenth wedding anniversary when a man wearing short-shorts and a tight polo shirt burst into the middle of the restaurant, placed his hands on his hips, and blew long and hard into a silver whistle. A thick gym rope unraveled from the ceiling and hung firmly above an exercise mat. "Listen up," he said, letting the whistle fall from his lips to dangle around his neck. "I don't want to hear any more excuses about being tired or hungry, being too old or out of shape, *or* that you're on your period," he said, eyeing a young woman who hid her head in her hands. "It's time to shape up or ship out." Lydia looked distressed and leaned toward me. "Mr. McKendrick let me go to the nurse's office last time. But I don't think he'll buy another stomachache," she said. "That rotten old bastard always gives me hell," I said. " I won't climb the rope this time," I said. "You will," said Lydia. "Okay, kids," said Mr. McKendrick. "Line up! Boys on one side, girls on the other." I kissed Lydia and joined the boys along the south wall. We all removed our dinner attire, hanging suits and gowns over chairs, to reveal matching P.E. uniforms. Mr. McKendrick blew his whistle again and shouted, "Hanson, you're up." I walked nervously toward the rope. "Come on Jeff, you can do it," shouted Lydia. "*Bullshit*," coughed Clyde Jenkins. "That's enough out of you, Jenkins. Alright, Hanson," said Mr. McKendrick, "let's see if you can get more than six inches off the ground this time." I looked up the rope and then all around me. The guys were cracking jokes and shouting things like, "*You'll never touch the sky, Hanson!*" and "*You just don't have it in you!*" "Come on, Hanson," said McKendrick, "before I'm so old I don't know my ass from a shoebox." I rubbed my hands together, grabbed the rope, and wrapped my legs around it. Then I pulled and I climbed and I pulled and I climbed and after several feet, I looked down at Lydia who had tears in her eyes. She blew me a kiss and waved me on, so I continued to climb. I kept expecting to reach the top, but after a while I looked down and there was nothing. Everyone and everything I'd ever known was gone. "Lydia!" I shouted into an echo. "Mr. McKendrick?" I didn't think I could climb down, so I just kept climbing up for what felt like hours, until I finally came

to the end of the line where the rope was tied around a boulder.
On the boulder sat a man who was cutting chunks off an apple with a knife and feeding himself with the blade. "What took you so long?" he said, without lifting his gaze. "I almost said to hell with it and cut the rope."

The Happy Pistoleer

I was visiting my sister in the country and awoke
in the middle of the night to the sound of gunfire. I went to the window
and saw my brother-in-law, Bart, shooting at the sky. I got dressed
and walked outside. He was just reloading his pistols when I arrived.
"Hey Bill," he said. "Sorry if I woke you." "It's alright," I said.
"I couldn't really sleep anyway. It's too dark. I'm not used to it."
"Want a beer?" he said. "Sure," I said. We sat down on a couple of
milk crates and sipped our beers. "Everything alright?" I said. "Sure,"
he said. "I just figured, I don't know, the guns, the beer, the middle
of the night, maybe something happened with Jessie." "Nope,"
he said. "We're right as rain." He sipped his beer and grimaced at the stars.
"So, what are you doing out here shooting at the sky?"
I said. "What do you mean?" he said. "Your sister never told you?"
"Told me what?" I said. "This is what I do," he said. "What you do?"
I said. "Yeah, Bill, this is what I *do*." "You get drunk and shoot
at the sky?" I said. "I can't believe she never told you," he said.
"Maybe she's embarrassed," I said. "No, you don't get it," he said.
"I make the stars." "You make stars?" I said. "No, man, *the* stars,"
he said, pointing to the sky. "You don't really think there are billions
of celestial bodies burning in the sky without any explanation as to how
and when they appeared, do you?" "That was my understanding," I said.
"This is ridiculous," he said, finishing his beer. "I bet you even believe
in God. I can't believe Jessie didn't say anything to you." He continued
reloading his pistols and cracked another beer. "What about the sky
art?" he said. "I suppose you think that's all just random, don't you?"
"You mean the constellations?" "No," he said, "I don't mean constellations,
I mean *sky art*. Hell, if you had any idea how long it takes me to make
just one of them, you'd sing a different tune." "What a bunch of malarkey,"
I said, opening another beer. "I'll prove it," he said as he cracked his knuckles.
"It's been ages since I had an audience anyway." He took out his pistols
and laughed giddily as he emptied their barrels into the sky. He shot them
one after another, reloaded, wiped sweat from his brow, cursed, reloaded,
laughed, drank more and more beer, reloaded, shot, and just as the sun
began to rise, he collapsed to the ground. There it was twinkling
in the sky, the fanned skin of a peeled banana, which for its shape could have

easily been mistaken for a starfish if not for the notable arch of a slipping foot.

The Mirepoix

"What are you making?" I said, walking into the kitchen. "A mirepoix," said Christina. "Really?" I said. "What's the occasion?" "I think it's time," said Christina. "That's too bad," I said. "I was really starting to like it here." "I was too," said Christina. "How do you want to do it?" I said, leaning on the counter. "Put on a record while I prepare everything?" "Alright," I said. I walked over to the record player and sifted through our collection. I watched Christina slice the carrots in half vertically and then into quarter-inch half-moons. "Did you find it?" "Got it," I said. I placed *Maiden Voyage* onto the turntable and rested the stylus upon the spinning record. Christina mowed through the celery without any consideration for its appearance. "It never gets enough credit, does it, the celery?" I said. Christina smiled and then lifted the onion to her nose and said, "What about Slippers?" "Forget about the cat," I said, taking the onion from her and placing it on the cutting board. Christina nodded in agreement and cut the ends off the onion with two swift motions. Then she punctured one side and peeled back the skin. I noticed her eyes begin to water, subtly at first, as if she were recalling a delicate history. As she divided the onion in half and proceeded to chop it into small chunks, the tears leaped from the bridge of her eyelids onto the cutting board. At one point she paused, put down the knife, and began to sob. "You have to finish," I said, crying hysterically. "I know, I know," she said, refusing to wipe her face. The tears were so voluminous that they began coating the floor. A salty film climbed the walls. As she sliced into the second half of the onion, the tears had flooded to our knees, the walls began to tremble, and the plaster ceilings cracked, crumbling sediment to the floor. We lost power and I heard the neighbors screaming in their homes. As Christina diced the final bits of onion, I took her in my arms and said, "I'll always love you."

The Zen Garden

For my birthday, Marianne bought me a miniature Zen garden. "I thought it would look nice in your office," she said. "Maybe over there by the orchid." "What fun," I said, placing it down on the shelf. "That's perfect." "The best part, though," said Marianne, "is that it comes with a tiny Buddhist monk." "What for?" I said. "He tends to the garden," she said, "so you don't have to. It says here on the box that every morning when you awaken, he'll have prepared a new design in the sand." "Wow," I said. "What'll they come up with next?" Marianne poured the sand into the tray, scattered the stones, arranged a pile of moss in the middle of the garden, then gently lifted the monk from his hermetic seal and placed him into the tray. He immediately lifted the rake and began drawing patterns into the sand. "Okay, well, I'm off to yoga," said Marianne. "Enjoy your garden." I sat down at my desk and watched the monk. Every twist and turn was patient and deliberate, and he never so much as sighed or grunted while he worked. By late afternoon he had arranged the stones in a delicate arch, raked quiet waves into the sand, and gathered the moss into a small heap where he sat meditating until nightfall. The next morning, he had moved the stones into the middle to create a high tower, carefully scattered the moss around it, and encircled the center in grooves of white sand. I showed Marianne when she came downstairs for coffee. "I'm glad you like it," she said. "It's remarkable," I said. For weeks I enjoyed the subtle shifting of the stones, the delicate rearrangement of moss, the tranquility in each fluid rift of sand. Then one morning I came downstairs and the monk had collected all the stones and moss to the far side and raked the sand into what appeared to be the image of a woman performing fellatio. The monk sat there quiet as ever, and didn't so much as budge even when I whispered to him, "Is that what I think it is?" I called Marianne into the room and said, "What does that look like to you?" Marianne looked closely and then said, "I think it's a flamingo." "Really," I said. "You don't see a woman going down on someone?" "No," said Marianne. "Of course not." "Alright," I said. "Must be my imagination." But the next day the monk had unmistakably drawn a couple having sex on a desk. The day after that was a woman being taken from behind. And the day after that she was riding a man like a cowgirl. By the following week I was convinced that Marianne was cheating on me. "I wouldn't do that to you," said Marianne, crying. "Well, how do you explain all the drawings?" I said. "Why would he rake all those pornographic images into the sand?" "I don't know," said Marianne. "Maybe he's a dirty monk." "You mean, like a dirty priest?" "Sure, why not?" "What sense does that make?" I said. "I don't know," she said, "but I wouldn't cheat on you. You have to believe me." "I want to believe you," I said. "But how can I trust you after all this?" "He must be crazy," she said. "He must be out of his mind. You have to believe me. You just *have* to." I poured us each a drink and about an hour later we were halfway through the bottle. We sat on the couch in my office watching television when a news report came on stating that Bigfoot had taken a lumberjack as a love slave, and that everyone should be wary about walking alone after dark. Halfway through the report, we started laughing out loud until we were both on the floor in tears. After a few minutes, Marianne said, "I feel like an animal." "Me too," I said. That's when we tore each other's clothes off and I took her from behind as we growled and bit each other. The next morning, we awoke covered in sweat and bloody scratches and passionately kissed. The monk lay on his back, dead in the sand, and it occurred to me that after all this time I never even thought to learn his name.

Mother

When I called Mother and she didn't answer, I turned to Heidi and said, "There's something fishy going on with Mother. She didn't answer the telephone." "Was she expecting your call?" said Heidi. "No," I said, "but she always answers." "It's not like you have a set time to talk every week, right?" said Heidi. "No, not really," I said, "but I've never needed to go to such lengths because she always answers the telephone." "What if she's in the shower?" said Heidi. "At two o'clock in the afternoon on a Saturday?" I said. "She probably stepped out to the store," said Heidi. "What store?" I said. "I don't know," said Heidi. "Maybe she needed milk or some new stockings." "You're not making any sense, Heidi," I said. "You're talking like a madwoman." "Get a hold of yourself," said Heidi. "Try her again in a few minutes and I'm sure she'll answer." Five minutes ticked by and then I dialed her telephone number again. It rang eight times and I hung up. "I'm going over there," I said. "Something's not right." "Are you sure you want to do that?" said Heidi. "I have to," I said. "I have to see her." "I'll drive you," said Heidi. I gave Heidi directions to Mother's in between gnawing on my fingernails and rocking impatiently in my seat. After about twenty minutes I shouted, "That's it. Pull in the driveway." I got out and ran to the door. Heidi stepped out of the car and leaned against it to wait. I rang the bell and banged on the door. "Mother? Mother, can you hear me?" A woman peeked out of the window through the curtains and opened the door with the chain still on. "Mother, thank God, I've been so worried," I said. "Why haven't you been answering the phone? I've been calling." "For the last time," she said. "I'm not your mother, you lunatic, and if you don't stop harassing me, I'm going to have to call the police." "The police? You're going to call the police on me. Fine," I said, "fuck you, Mother!"

Let It Snow

"Richard, where are you going?" said Shelly. "Where do you *think* I'm going?" I said. "No," she said, "you can't." "I have to," I said. "No, you don't," said Shelly. "You can stay here with me and the children. You can stay home." "You know it's not that easy," I said. "Of course, it is," said Shelly. "Just sit down, eat dinner with us, and talk about your day. It's that simple." "I can't do that anymore," I said. "Don't you understand? There's something out there. There's reason to believe our world could turn upside down at any given moment. I can't just sit here anymore pretending everything's normal." "Please," said Shelly, "just one more night." "I'm sorry," I said. "I have to go." I grabbed my knapsack and threw it over my shoulder. "Listen," I said, opening the door, "it's going to be alright." Shelly grabbed my arm and kissed my hand as I headed out into the settled snow. "Come back to us," said Shelly before closing the door behind me. I walked down the road where streetlights stood on either side, illuminated with a glossy finish. The neighborhood cars parked in the driveways were like smudges of paint. Even the trees, which I swear I climbed as a child, seemed as if they were constructed out of straw. "Hey Dick," said Eddie, running up behind me. "Hey Eddie," I said. "Thanks for coming." "Thanks nothing, man, I'm just as curious as you are," he said. "How did Lola take it?" I said. "Hell, brother, you know Lola, can't have a conversation that doesn't end like a shaken soda," said Eddie. "I'm sorry," I said. "I would've gone alone." "Don't worry about it," said Eddie, patting my back. We walked along the road in the intermittent darkness when Eddie said, "So have you thought about what we'll do if it happens again?" "There's no *if*," I said. "It'll happen again, it's just a question of when." "Well, *when* it happens again, what are we going to do?" "I don't know," I said. "Have you thought about what it is?" said Eddie. "Earthquake maybe, something to do with the Earth's gravitational pull," I said. "Whatever it is, last time it happened I was sitting on the john and, well, shit," said Eddie. "Shelly and I were making love," I said, smirking. "It certainly made things a little more interesting." We finally reached the end of town and Eddie slammed his head and fell to the ground. "What in the world?" said Eddie. "What happened?" I said. "What did you hit?" "Nothing, man," said Eddie. "Not a damn thing." I reached in front of me and my hands flattened against glass. "What's going on?" I stammered. I started feeling all around the glass as it arched upward into the sky. I kicked away the snow and found that the glass was completely embedded into the earth. "Help me up," said Eddie. I got him to his feet and dusted the snow from his clothes. Just then a light came on in the sky. "I thought it was night," I said. "It was," said Eddie. "That's impossible." We noticed movement in the beyond and then Eddie yelled, "Run!" He took off down the road, but I ran to the nearest tree and held onto its two-dimensional trunk. An enormous hand eclipsed the light and unearthed the entire town from the ground. The hand brought us closer and closer to a young face, no older than my youngest daughter, and she, with a joyfully devilish smile, vigorously shook the world. Snow whipped in all directions and screams bellowed from the unmoving houses and cars. Eddie was lifted clean off his feet and smashed his head against the top of the world, falling to his death in a heap. I held onto the tree thinking of Shelly and the children, my hands bloody and aching for peace. Finally, the hand placed us down and I could hear the voices, young and old, celebrating the beauty of our small town. Then someone started singing, "Let it snow! Let it snow! Let it snow!" before we were once again lifted and shaken, and it would take far too long for the snow to finally settle.

The Supermarket

I was standing in line at the supermarket waiting to check out when the man in front of me removed a pair of clippers from his pocket and began clipping his fingernails onto the conveyor belt. "Excuse me," I said, "but should you be doing that here?" "Doing what?" he said. "You're clipping your fingernails onto the conveyor belt," I said. "Oh, was I?" he said. "Yes," I said. "I beg your pardon," he said. "I didn't realize." Then he went right on clipping his fingernails. When he finished, he covered his face in shaving cream, gently drew a razor over his cheek, and tapped it off onto the credit card pad. "Pardon me," I said. "What makes you think you can do that here?" "Do what?" he said. "You're shaving," I said. "Was I shaving?" he said as he continued to shave his face and neck. "You still are," I said. "Me, shaving, I don't think so," he said, tapping bits of hair and cream all over the place. The cashier scanned his clipped fingernails and the gobs of shaving cream and bagged them as best she could. "You don't find it disgusting, or at least rude, to groom yourself in public?" "You know, you've got some nerve, buddy," he said as he removed his clothing and poured a gallon of water over his head before massaging shampoo into his scalp. I turned to the woman behind me and said, "Are you seeing this?" She looked at me, averting her eyes from the bathing man. "Pervert," she said. "Mind your own business." The cashier was busily bagging the soapy suds as he brushed his teeth and spit his foamy saliva into her hands. "Price check on foamy saliva," said the cashier into the intercom. "Price check on foamy saliva." Then he poured more water over himself and began to inspect his face, popping pimples and noting his hairline. He must have noticed me staring at him in horror, because he looked right into my eyes and said, "Can't a guy go to the store without being harassed anymore?" before he soaped up his torso, rummaged through my cart, and sang into my perfectly ripened eggplant.

A New Man

I don't know what inspired me to follow the man home.
Maybe it was the way he nervously ran his fingers through his hair
contemplating women's deodorant. Maybe it was how he
sighed standing in front of the contraceptives, and once more at
the hair loss remedies. It could have been how he perused
the potato chips, slapped his fat belly, and took a few steps away.
Then, having second thoughts, he returned, grabbed two family-sized
bags and rushed to the cashier before he had a chance to talk himself
out of it. I passed him on the way to my car where I waited for him
to leave. He climbed into a rusty hatchback and turned over the lethargic
ignition. I followed him west on Porter into a little subdivision
with cookie-cutter houses. I parked a few houses down after he pulled
into his driveway and waddled into his home. A few minutes later
I walked up to the front door and rang the bell. I heard him grumble
before unlatching the chain and opening the door. "Can I help you?"
he said. "I like your house," I said. He looked at me crossly and said,
"Don't mess with me. I've had a very long day." "I'm not," I said.
"I wouldn't do that." He looked me up and down. "Are you sure?"
he said. "Yes," I said. "I really, really like your house." Then he pushed
open the screen door and stepped outside. "Thank God," he said.
"You can have it, my whole life. It's all yours." He handed me the keys
to the house, grabbed a coat, walked down the driveway, and disappeared
down the road. I stepped inside just as a woman yelled, "Dinner!"
Two kids ran down the stairs. The boy ran passed me and said,
"Hey Dad!" The older one, the girl, stopped in front of me and looked me
over. "You look weird," she said. "New haircut?" "Felix," shouted
the woman. "Come to the table before your food gets cold." I took off
my shoes and walked to the dining room. I sat down at the head
of the table and looked at my new family. The kids loudly teased
each other and threw mashed potatoes back and forth. My wife
unwrapped an apron from her rather globular figure and sat down
across from me. "Felix," she said, "that new face cream must be doing you
wonders. You look radiant, like a new man." "I feel like a new man,"
I said, softly winking at her. I complimented her rose-patterned dress
and insisted the meatloaf sauce had the perfect ratio of sweetness and spice,

which made her blush and giggle. And after subtly flirting over a dessert of scrumptious apple cobbler, she undid the top two buttons of her dress, and suggested in a rather sultry tone that we leave the dishes for morning and go immediately to bed.

Kissing Dynamite

"Russ," said Vickie. "My parents will be here any minute." "Alright," I said, folding my newspaper and setting it on the desk. I walked into the living room. "How's our little bundle of joy?" I said, wrapping my arms around Vickie as she stared into the bassinet. "She's perfect," said Vickie, leaning in to kiss her. A few minutes later we heard a gentle knocking at the door. "That must be my parents," said Vickie. We went through the usual pleasantries and then Vickie's mother Cheryl said, "Well, I didn't come all this way just for hugs and kisses. Show me that baby." "Let's hope she takes after her mother, huh, Russ?" said Vickie's father, Owen, elbowing me in the ribs. "We can only hope," I said, putting on a smile. "She's in the living room," said Vickie, "but she's very temperamental." "You were always a bit of a sparkler yourself," said Cheryl. "Don't you remember, Owen?" "Sparkler, nothing," he said. "She was like the Fourth of July." "*Daddy*," said Vickie. "I'm sorry," said Owen, "but it's true." We walked into the living room and Owen and Cheryl leaned over the bassinet. "Is this some kind of joke?" said Owen. "What do you mean?" I said. "Vickie, honey, you told us over the phone you had a baby, a real honest-to-goodness baby," said Owen. "We do," said Vickie, rushing over to the bassinet and lifting the baby to her chest. "Oh dear," said Cheryl. "I thought just for once, maybe this time we'd get back on track." "Forget it," said Owen, "we should have known that Russ couldn't get the job done." "Daddy, that's not fair," said Vickie. "Russ is a wonderful husband and father." "But he couldn't even give you a baby." "You know what, Owen, you really are a giant sack of shit," I said. "I've been telling you for years, I'm a giant sack of ammonium nitrate," he said, angrily brushing white pellets off his woven polypropylene slacks. "I just wish you could love her regardless of her appearance," said Vickie. "That's a stick of dynamite, not a baby," said Owen. "She's *our* baby," said Vickie, crying. "She'll be loved and supported and become anything she wants to be!" "You're delusional," said Owen. "Everybody calm down," I said. "Why did we expect anything more from a hand grenade like Russ?" said Cheryl. "That's rich coming from you, Cheryl, you're like a heat-seeking missile for the latest opinion," I said. "Stop, just stop it!" said Vickie. "At least we accepted that you were a firecracker, Vickie," said Cheryl. "We never once wanted you to be anything else."

The Disappearing Act

In the morning when I reached for my glasses, they weren't on the nightstand where I'd left them. Then I rolled over to cuddle with Stacy, but she, too, was missing. I scooched back to my side, sat up, and planted my feet on the floor. "Honey, have you seen my slippers?" I shouted. I rubbed my eyes and, hearing no reply, stood and stretched, went to the bathroom, looked everywhere for my toothbrush, and then walked downstairs for a cup of coffee. When I got to the kitchen the coffee pot was gone, along with my favorite mug. "Stacy, where's the coffeemaker? Where's my mug?" I said. "And where are you?" I drank a glass of water instead, yawned, and walked back upstairs to take a shower. When I finished washing up, I reached for my towel, but that also seemed to be elsewhere. I dried myself with Stacy's half-wet towel, ignored the absence of my deodorant and razor, and went to my closet to get dressed, but all my clothes had vanished. "Stacy, what happened to my clothes? What's going on?" I shouted wearily. She didn't answer. I even looked for the pajamas I had just worn and they had also disappeared. I walked naked into the living room and noticed that all my records, books, knickknacks, in fact, everything I owned was simply gone. "Stacy, honey, help me. Something's terribly wrong." After a few minutes of panic and self-loathing, I picked up the telephone and dialed the police department. "Officer," I said, "I'd like to report a robbery. All my belongings have disappeared and I'm left standing naked in my kitchen. Also, my wife is nowhere to be found." "Are any of your wife's belongings missing?" he said. "Not that I can tell," I said, looking around. "That doesn't sound like a robbery," he said. "It sounds to me like you're dying." "Dying?" I said. "Sure," he said. "It's a classic case of pre-mortem disintegration." "Have you seen this kind of thing before?" I said. "Couple times a day, easy," he said. "Most victims don't even realize it's coming. One day you've lost your keys, or a pair of socks, then it's a toothbrush, a favorite piece of furniture, and after that it doesn't take very long to discover that your whole life has turned to smoke. It's just the universe's way of taking care of things, I suppose." "Wow," I said. "How long do I have?" "The disappearing act is different for everyone," he said, "but I'm sure you'll be vanishing soon enough." "How am I supposed to tell my wife?" I said. "Oh, I wouldn't worry too much about that," he said. "Most spouses see this sort of thing coming. I'm sure she's already planned your funeral, put your house up for sale. Heck, she's probably even taken a new lover. They always do."

A Wonderful World

On the radio this morning, the newsman reported that civilization was returning to nature. Apparently, nature had suffered humanity long enough and was launching a revolution. The police received phone calls about houseplants attacking homeowners, pets being swallowed up by bushes and tall grass, and even trees uprooting themselves and terrorizing the city. "We'll issue further reports," said the newsman, "for as long as nature allows. After that, may God be with us all." I turned down Walnut Street, or at least what used to be Walnut Street. The road signs were all replaced by saplings and shrubs, roots had busted up the roads, and a herd of buffalo had stopped to graze in the thicket. I slowly weaved between them and continued my commute to work even while I noticed that many of the trees were overturning vehicles and chasing frantic pedestrians. One threw apples at children in a schoolyard, while another set fire to its limbs and dove through the bay window of a department store. I pulled over at a coffee shop on 14th Street where I usually stopped for an espresso, but it was completely overrun with cicadas. When I turned back to my car, a rhinoceros had blasted it to pieces, so I started walking to the office. The grass on either side of the sidewalk started clawing at my loafers and a beautiful rosebush lashed out against my legs and arms, drawing blood. Once I reached the park I took out my cell phone and called the office. "Kevin, it's Dale." "Dale, my God where are you? We're trapped in the office. The dandelions are trying to get in, my God, the dandelions. You've got to do something. Call someone!" I hung up the phone. Then I removed my clothing and walked into the park. I covered myself in mud and my own feces and took a nap by a giant boulder. When I awoke there was a naked woman lying next to me. We looked at each other and, having completely forgotten our language, grunted as if to say "*Oh, what a wonderful world.*"

The Medicine Cabinet

Lorrie was having difficulty with the bathroom mirror. She gently tugged on the left side, then the right. She looked for a split down the middle, anything to indicate an opening. After a few minutes she came out of the bathroom drying her hands with a towel. "What's wrong with your bathroom mirror?" she said. "What do you mean?" I said. "Look at it," she said. I put down the magazine I was reading and walked over to the bathroom. "Seems fine to me," I said. "It doesn't want to open," she said. "What does it want to do?" I said. "It just wants to be a mirror, I guess," she said. "Hasn't it always been a mirror?" I said. "Probably, but I thought it was also a medicine cabinet," she said. "I don't know," I said. "It's never been a medicine cabinet before." "Are you sure?" she said. "I think so," I said. "Why do you want to get in there so badly?" "They say it's a great way to get to know someone," she said. "You can ask me anything," I said. "Medicine cabinets don't keep secrets," she said. "If you really want to make this relationship work, you're going to have to open that mirror." Even though I hadn't yet told her I loved her, I knew that I did, so I went to the garage and got a pair of gloves and a crowbar and a couple of headlamps. When I got back to the bathroom, Lorrie had finally found a weakness in the mirror. I kneeled on top of the vanity and wedged the crowbar in. I pulled with all my strength but it wouldn't budge. I took off my shirt, wiped the sweat from my brow and tried again. This time, she too climbed up on the vanity and wrapped her arms around me, and together we pried open the mirror. We turned on our headlamps and crawled inside. In the distance was a desert. A firing squad took aim at a gagged and blindfolded man tied to a tree. A couple of laughing soldiers held back a woman who screamed, "*Jonny my love, not my Jonny!*". "Why is he wearing a paper target?" asked Lorrie. "They try to avoid disfigurement," I said, "by aiming at the heart." The soldiers raised their weapons, fired, and Jonny's body slumped over. The woman was freed and she ran to him and took him in her arms, ruining her beautiful white dress. "He never got his cigarette," I said. "At least they could have given him a lousy cigarette." That's when Lorrie took my hand in hers and I knew we'd be together forever.

A Bottomless Freefall

I dialed the number in the "Help Wanted" section of this morning's paper. The man on the other end of the line sounded nervous, stammering as he spoke. "H-h-hello?" he said. "I'm calling about the job," I said. "You'll have to be more specific," he said. "The one about slapping you every few minutes to make sure you're awake." "Yes, yes of course," he said. "It's a very important job, requiring unwavering commitment. Do you have any experience?" "I used to break windows in my dreams like an explosion of larks." "That's very enticing," he said, "but have you ever thought unforgivingly of moonlight on a white nightgown, or pitied a narcoleptic vampire?" "I like to think I'm a viper in the throat of a bottomless freefall, and what's more, I have very strong hands," I said. "Soft but strong, or so I've been told. Imagine fire gently stroking your face, or falling asleep in the cab of a streetcleaner." "You sound perfect," he said, "just what I've been looking for, but how do I know you're real?" "Hit yourself over the head with your telephone," I said. "Are you sure that'll work?" he said. "It's worked before," I said, "but you best do it a few times to be sure." "Alright," he said. "Please hold." The man on the line hit himself over and over again. I could hear the collision of the receiver against his skull. After several minutes he said, "Wow! You're really good, and by all accounts you must be real, really and truly real." "As real as the space between us," I said, "or the breath of someone who's trying desperately to find you."

A Gentlemen's Club

       I was walking one hot summer day when I passed by a gentlemen's club. There was a sign outside depicting a beautiful woman shyly covering her breasts with one hand and blowing a kiss with the other. "What the hell," I said aloud to myself. I paid the entry fee and walked inside. I went into a private room and paid for the curtain to open. I expected music to play, something that might inspire someone to take off their clothing, but instead it was the theme music from *I Love Lucy*. As the curtain parted, there was an elderly man sitting on a couch weeping. He took a sip of lemonade and removed his sweater, shoes and socks. He sighed and looked at his wristwatch. Then he blew his nose with an embroidered handkerchief and the curtain closed. I paid more money and the curtain reopened. The man hunched over a TV dinner, belching and farting, and looked at a black-and-white photograph of a young woman leaning against a convertible with a big smile on her face. "Millie, oh Millie," I heard him whisper. He pressed the photograph to his chest, pushed away his dinner, and lit a cigarette. He stood, removed his pants, and danced with the photograph, occasionally stopping to kiss it. Then the curtain closed. I paid again and the curtain reopened. The man was waltzing and sobbing. Finally, he stumbled and clutched his chest before he violently spasmed and fell to the floor, lifeless. His eyes parted slightly to catch my reaction. "I'm afraid to close my eyes," I said. "I think it means I'm waking up." The curtain closed just as I heard Ricky threatening to spank Lucy for spending their bill money on a new mink stole.

The Carolers

We had just finished dinner and were settling down by the fire. Pamela was getting a blanket from the chest when the doorbell rang. She tossed the blanket over the arm of the couch and looked out the window. "Jim!" she said, in a rather frantic tone. "Carolers." "Alright," I said, putting down my tea on the coffee table and grabbing a sweater. "I'll answer the door and keep them busy," said Pamela. "Okay," I said. "Be right there." Pamela opened the door and the carolers broke out into song. Pamela stood there smiling and clapping along as a cold breeze swept passed her and into the house. "Jim, hurry up," she hollered. "You're missing the show." I rushed toward the door with a box full of cutout cookies decorated with frosting and sprinkles. "Cookies," I shouted over the caroling. "Everyone get your Christmas cookies." The carolers accepted the offering and started mumbling through stuffed mouths. "There's plenty more where that came from," I said, leading them away from the house and out into the yard. A few carolers began to dance in the moonlight. Others made snow angels or looked up at the stars. I had just finished giving out the last of the cookies when I heard the screeching of tires. Three large men with nets and flashlights leaped out of a white van. The carolers didn't seem to notice at first, but eventually one saw the flashlights and started running. Then the first net came down, followed by another, and another. A few of the younger carolers leaped the fence and ran off into the neighborhood. When the rest were detained, one of the men said, "Thank you, sir, you did the right thing." "You're not going to hurt them are you?" I said as I watched the carolers being wrangled into the van. "No, nothing like that. We always try give them a chance, find them good homes with loving families. There's always someone looking to adopt, especially this time of year." "That's wonderful," I said. "I'm happy to hear that." "Of course, there's usually a few that are just plain unlovable and have to get put down, but nine times out of ten those are the ones that can't carry a tune to save their lives anyway."

The Adventures of Martin George

for Russel Edson

It had been three weeks since the radio program
began narrating my every move without commercial break.
One evening, Jenny playfully twisted my left nipple
and there came the snowy sound of channels reaching
for reception. She let go almost immediately, but nonetheless
a voice came booming through my chest. *"We now present
The Adventures of Martin George."* We found it amusing
at first, listening to the narrator describe our activities
in the bedroom, noticing how washing the dishes became somehow
whimsical under the direction of my baritone possessor.
But after several weeks of hearing him describe every detail
of our lives, no matter how mundane, private, or grotesque,
it began to drive us mad. One morning Jenny dropped her fork
onto her plate and shouted, "Martin, I can't take it anymore!"
The narrator described how she threw her arms in the air
as if she were discarding her final shred of patience, and began
weeping like the slow trickle of a spring rain upon the quiet slats
of an uninhabited farmhouse. "I love you, but I don't need to know
every little thing about you. There are just some things in a marriage
that require mystery." "What am I supposed to do?" I said,
as the narrator instructed me to frustratedly run my fingers
through my hair. "I don't know, but we need some semblance
of privacy," said Jenny. "Maybe we can try turning off the radio?
We never tried the right nipple." "We talked about this,"
I said. "What if in turning off my right nipple it turns me off
altogether?" "We've tried everything else," said Jenny. "We either
twist your right nipple or, I'm sorry, but I'm going to have to leave."
"That's so unreasonable," I said. "You have to see how
difficult this is for me." "I do, I think," said Jenny. "I just can't
live this way anymore and you shouldn't either." *"Martin placed
his head in his hands as he paced back and forth,"* said the narrator,
*"and thought in great depth about the decision he was about to make.
He would either face possible death or lose the woman he loves. It was as if
his recurring dream of love cascaded through his heart like
an unmanned skiff floating down the Ohio River."*

Glowing

An old man had fallen on some loose gravel in the grocery store parking lot and was struggling to get to his feet. I rushed over to him, set down my bags, and gently helped him up. His forehead was bleeding and his chin was badly gashed. "Thank you, my boy," said the old man. "God bless you." "You're bleeding," I said, removing a handkerchief from my pocket and pressing it to his forehead. "Oh, I'll be alright," said the old man. I looked him over and noticed his chin resembled a cracked windshield and there was a faint light emerging from the blemished web. "Your chin," I said. "It appears to be...glowing." The old man looked elated. "Are you sure?" he said, dropping the handkerchief to the ground and feeling for the shattered flesh. "Pretty sure," I said. "We probably ought to get you to a hospital." "No need," he said as he removed his coat and tossed it aside. "I'll be alright." "Well, can I call someone to come get you?" He ignored me and feverishly began to peel away the shards on his chin and toss them onto the pavement. "I don't really think you should be messing with that," I said, attempting to help him. He slapped my hands away, scattering bloody tissue everywhere. With every fragment removed, more light poured from his face. It became so blinding I had to cover my eyes. Then came a cracking like the magnified emergence of a primordial reptile from its shell. I watched as he discarded pieces of his body like wet carboard onto the heated cement— nose, ears, followed by scalp and eyes until the rest of his body splashed to the ground in a steamy puddle at my feet. The light extinguished and as my eyes readjusted, I watched a bearded dragon wiggle free from his trousers. It raised its head into the sun, caught the scent of a small rodent, and quickly skidded away between the shuffling legs of afternoon shoppers.

The Player Piano

"It's time," said a young woman who sat next to me on the bus. "Time for what?" I said, looking at my wristwatch. "Time for the baby," she said, removing her pants and underwear before squatting down over the slush-soaked floorboards. "It's coming!" she yelled. The man to my left looked at me, disgusted. "Aren't you going to help your wife?" he said. "Things aren't the way they used to be, you know." "She's not my wife," I said. "Then you ought to make an honest woman out of her," he said. "My mother was a single parent and believe you me, it's no picnic." "But she and I have never even met before," I said, gesturing to the woman who huffed and puffed over her broken water. "Cold feet," said an older woman clutching a bag of groceries. "My husband had cold feet too, but we've been married almost fifty years now." "That's wonderful," I said. "Congratulations." The laboring woman groaned, grabbed my leg and dragged me to her side. "That man over there is a priest," said another man pointing a rolled-up newspaper at a man in the back. "Father, this lovely couple would like to be married," shouted a young woman. "I don't think I'm ready for marriage and children," I said. "No one's ever ready for marriage and children," said the bus driver over the intercom, "but it happens whether we like it or not." The priest opened his Bible and performed the ceremony. No one objected, and all the passengers applauded. The young woman squeezed my hand, looked into my eyes, and said, "There's no one I'd rather be with than you." "I love you," I said, and I think I meant it. Then the bus pulled over at the next stop and a homeless man ran down the aisle to kneel down between the quivering legs of my bride. "We're going to need one more really good push," he said. "I can't," she said. "I'm so tired." "You can do it," I said, kissing her on the forehead. "You're the strongest person I've ever known and our baby is so lucky to have you as its mother." She kissed my hand and took a deep breath. Then she pushed with all her might, and I thought I heard the sound of depressed piano keys in the distance. "It's coming," said the homeless man. My lovely wife groaned once more and finally, the baby was born. The homeless man held it by its legs, slapped its lid, and music began to cry out. "It's a player piano," I said. "It looks just like you," said my wife, playing a major pentatonic along my tearful cheek.

History

I walked out of the post office and there was a man on his hands and knees licking the cobblestone sidewalk. He turned around to look at me. "Lots of history here," he said. "Did you know our town was founded by a man named Herbert Whitlock?" "I'm afraid not," I said. "He never got any credit on account of his deformity." "That's unfortunate," I said. "Sure is," he said, before he continued vigorously licking. I continued on my way and stopped in front of an antique shop where I once looked for a brooch for Tina. Through the window I watched a young woman passionately kissing an old iron doorstopper, half a dozen men rubbing their bare chests on a large bronze statue of a griffin, and numerous others fondling various vintage items. I saw an original Singer sewing machine and felt an urge to pierce my flesh with its needle, but I quickly cleared my mind and continued walking. On the corner of Jefferson and Lafayette, traffic had stalled for an elderly woman who was lying face down in the road. I ran up to her, got down on my knees, and asked, "Are you alright?" The woman turned her head and smiled. "This is where I was conceived 89 years ago today," she said, inhaling deeply. "It also happens to be the very place where many fought and died in the Battle of Foghorn." "I've never heard of it," I said. "It was covered up by the town magistrate in 1842, but you can still smell it regardless of how many times they repave." I continued on and took a shortcut through a residential neighborhood where many children had gathered on their front lawns. Some were weeping, others worriedly sharing stories of their parents. "My father won't come out of the dumbwaiter," said a distraught young girl. "Mine has laughed himself to tears straddling a Dutch door," said a scruffy boy. "Our grandfather keeps scraping his boots on the boot scraper, and now the soles of his feet are bloody and raw," whimpered a set of twins. "Why won't my mother stop fingering the mail slot and staring blankly at the transom windows?" said another. When I arrived home I called for Tina. "Up here," she said. I ran upstairs to tell her about everything I saw and found her naked, attempting to wedge herself into the laundry chute beneath the sink. "What are you doing?" I said. "Life is a never-ending chore," she said. "And besides, I've always wanted to know what it feels like to be a soiled blouse descending as fast as possible in complete secrecy."

Linus

Linus and I walked down to the beach for a game
of fetch. "Go get it!" I shouted as I threw a stick
for him and watched him dart off across the sand.
He carried it back more slowly than usual and
seemed to be hobbling. "What do you have, boy?"
He dropped his left hind leg at my feet and barked
as if he expected me to throw it. I took it in my hand,
so delicate and soft, and pitched it out across the
dunes. He barked and chased after it. When he returned,
he was dragging himself by his front legs and carrying both
hind legs clutched between his jaws. He dropped
them at my feet and barked. I lifted them, holding
his paws in my hands. Then I tossed them, much closer
this time, and watched him drag his body after them.
He retrieved them and pulled himself forward
with only his front right leg. When he reached me, he opened
his jaws and let his legs fall out. He barked and whined
and so I lifted his legs, turned around, and simply
dropped them. He slowly circled me, losing his final
leg and began to bark and thrash in the sand.
"Sweet boy," I said. Then I kicked off my shoes,
lifted him and his legs to my chest and walked
into the sea. After the first wave, I set him down
and watched him wiggle off into the frothy surf.
I watched him leap from the water and bark
at me as I stood there waving. After a few
minutes he disappeared, leaving me with his legs.
Not knowing what else to do in that moment,
I began to juggle them, tossing them higher and
higher into the sky until at once they appeared to
embark on a restless, and self-torturing spiritual
quest, agile and lucid and so very glad to be alive.

Acknowledgements

All my love to Emily for your love and support, for believing in me and encouraging this work.

Thank you to my children Henry, Hattie, and Huxley for requesting I read you poems before bed every night. I love you beyond words.

Thank you to Sarah Elkins for enduring my rants and loving this project even when I didn't, and for your early editorial suggestions.

Thank you Andrew K. Peterson, Jared Hayes, and Tim Armentrout for your years of friendship and poetry.

Thank you to Ted Chin for allowing me to use your amazing visual art for the book cover.

Finally, thank you to Freddy La Force and Vegetarian Alcoholic Press for taking on this manuscript and to Janae Mancheski for your incredible editorial guidance. This book would not appear in this form without your attention to detail and your continued devotion.

www.ingramcontent.com/pod-product-compliance
Lightning Source LLC
Chambersburg PA
CBHW060535080526
44586CB00012B/743